# The Village of
# Shalmsford, Kent
## 1841-1891

a family history resource

by

## Susan Hibberd

with illustrations by Colin McGowan

©Susan Hibberd 2017

This book is sold subject to the condition that it shall not, by way of trade or otherwise, be lent, resold, hired out, or otherwise circulated without the publisher's prior consent in any form of binding or cover other than that in which it is published and without a similar condition including this condition being imposed on the subsequent publisher.

The moral right of Susan Hibberd has been asserted.

ISBN 978-0-956665683

First published in Great Britain in 2017
Butterfly Cottage Publishing
87 Shalmsford Street,
Chartham, Kent, CT4 7RN

# Introduction

If you wake up with the sunrise, the sound of the dawn chorus echoing in your ears and look out of an upstairs window in Mersham Villas (91-93 Shalmsford Street), the view will be almost the same as that seen by the people living in Shalmsford during the reign of Queen Victoria. With the notable exception of the railway line, the countryside around the hamlet has changed remarkably little over the past 180 years.

There are more houses, and the occasional car, but in the very early morning, it is easy to feel the ghosts of those who lived, worked and died in the village still reluctant to leave. The field boundaries remain much the same, stretching out on either side of you towards the comforting bulk of the hills which surround the floodplain of the River Stour, and the village retains its separate identity as a rural hamlet, cut off from other villages, including Chartham, by field and river.

Shalmsford would have been a sleepy village, were it not for the fact that it lies on the main toll road from Ashford to Canterbury. The River Stour was a huge impediment to horse-drawn carts, wagons and carriages, with its wide margin of water meadows, so the main road from Ashford to Canterbury crossed the river at Shalmsford, travelled uphill away from the mud and then turned down Cockering Road, before winding through Larkey Valley down into Wincheap, missing the nearby village of Chartham altogether. All the traffic between Ashford and Canterbury therefore passed through Shalmsford, bringing goods, mail and a regular supply of gossip. The mail coach passed through at least once each day, manned by an armed guard carrying a custlass, a brace of pistols and a blunderbuss. Tolls were collected at Shalmsford Bridge Cottage, the last house in the parish of Chilham.

When the railway was built in the late 1840s, the A28 Ashford to Canterbury Road was built and Shalmsford lost a part of itself. Travel became easier, jobs were to be found in the city instead of locally, and the tight-knit community spirit of the village loosened.

However, Shalmsford still retains its own identity, distinct from Chartham, and villagers are proud to call it their home. The road sign on the A28 shows 'Shalmsford Street' as a separate destination from Chartham, the area had its own pub until very recently, and although the chapel and the Salvation Army Hall have now closed, leaving St Mary's in Chartham as the main centre of religion, Shalmsford has kept the area Post Office. Both the school and the two doctor's surgeries also fall outside Chartham village, but within that of Shalmsford. Even the Parish Design Statement recognises that Shalmsford Street is a distinct settlement, along with Mystole, Chartham Hatch and St Augustine's.

The rapid growth of rural communities during the Victorian period was staggering, and the tiny hamlet of Shalmsford is a perfect example of how working class villages in Kent responded to this growth.

When Queen Victoria came to the throne in 1837, Shalmsford was still very much a separate settlement from Chartham Village, but by the end of her reign in 1901, is had, administratively at least, become part of Chartham Village as a it is today.

For the purposes of this study, I shall be looking at the district of Shalmsford, which falls into the second census enumeration category. This area varied slightly during the seven censuses that were taken by the Victorians (1841-1901), but it generally encompassed Bolts Hill, Shalmsford Street, Pickleden, Mystole, Upperdown and Thruxted.

In the early Victorian period, the housing on Shalmsford Street petered out at Bolts Hill, where the homes followed the road down the hill towards Chartham Green. The upper end of the street wasn't developed until the late Victorian period, following the building of the Asylum in 1875. At the bottom of the hill a large area of water meadow skirts a tributary of The Stour, passing The Deanery and its associated outbuildings. This is the end of the hamlet of Shalmsford.

The Ashford to Canterbury Railway, built through Chilham and Chartham to avoid the North Downs, passes through the very centre of the village and was opened in 1846, although the people of Chartham voted not to have a railway station at this time. Their link to the railway was been limited to complaining about the noise and the soot while the children waved at the passing trains and played too near the lines. There would also have been complaints about the behaviour of the 'navvies' while the railroad was being built. Multiple accounts record their poor behaviour and the way they were often found drunk and fighting after work. However, landlords Thomas Newington at 'The Cross Keys' and Jesse Hukins at 'The George' may have been glad of the business.

The railway company extracted gravel from the Gravel Pit opposite numbers 65-81 Shalmsford Street, and it is still a low-lying are, prone to flooding but home to some threatened wildlife such as the cuckoo and certain toads.

Information about the daily lives of these families has been lost in time, but I found *'How to be a Victorian'* by Ruth Goodman to be an excellent indicator of the lives of ordinary people.

Shalmsford is still the home of ordinary people, and as you read this study, I think you will find that our lives are not that different from those of the people who came before us.

My thanks go to all those who have helped, in particular local residents Julie Hoare, Mick Gipson and Neil Campbell and co-opted editor-in-chief Judith Charles.

I hope you enjoy getting to know the people who went before as much as I did.

*Susan*

# The 1840s

The winter of 1840/41 was particularly harsh, and the people of Shalmsford were glad to see the first signs of spring when it came.

Residents will have remembered 1839 as a particularly wet year (the county had 150% of its annual rainfall between June and November) although 1840 was very dry. This swing between wet and dry presaged a time of uncertainty in the weather which eventually culminated in the Potato Famine in Ireland, the fallout from which was felt all across the UK.

This was the decade that saw the landscape change forever by the introduction of bridges instead of fords across the River Stour. Selina Randolph in her book of 1911 describes how The Stour ran from below Pickledon, by ford across the bottom of Port Fields, north to Shalmsford Bridge, then through Deanery Meadow, and across Flower Show Meadow by the Rectory Gardens, at a time when the current river from the Corn Mill to the Rectory was but a stream.

The tithe map of Chartham from 1839, shows roads, dwellings and field boundaries. The map was drawn up to show the rateable value of land as tithe payments changed from a requirement to pay 1/10 of produce to a monetary value. It is interesting to note that many of the field boundaries are still visible in the landscape today, being retained as property boundaries, hedgerows or footpaths.

Another interesting fact is the speed with which families move around. It is a temptation to think of Victorian country life as being slow and measured, but the names on the tithe map of 1839 do not tally with those on the census of 1841; people have moved. The rented houses were frequently given to workers as part of their wage, so when they ceased the work, their home was forfeit. Thus, they often moved, and having few possessions, this was no great hardship, for they very usually stayed in the same village or at least in the same general area.

## The 1841 Census

The Victorians continued the system of taking a national census every ten years with which had been started in 1801, but it was extended in 1841 to record the details of every person in the country.

The first census, was taken on night of 6th June 1841 and compiled by a series of local enumerators. Each household was required to complete a return and the enumerator copied the information into the Census Enumeration Book. The forms were given out on a Sunday and the enumerator returned the next day to collect the completed forms. He was also empowered to help fill in the forms, should anyone need it, as the literacy rate in the country was only a little over 50% at this time.

For this census, the ages of children under fifteen were recorded accurately, but for those over this age, the figure was rounded down to the nearest five. Thus, someone who was 26 was recorded as 25, which is not too far off. However, a person who was 29 would also be recorded as being 25, which is a significant difference. A detailed inspection of the original pages of the enumeration books can sometimes give an indication of real age, where the correct age has been entered and subsequently altered.

The occupation of children was not generally recorded, perhaps because parents were embarrassed about having to rely on this income to survive. A child who worked as an agricultural labourer would work from 7am until 6pm and would expect to earn anything from 4d to 10d depending on the type of work undertaken, averaging out at approximately two shillings a week. The work included stone picking, weeding, bird scaring or light field work such as planting. The stones picked from the fields were used on the roads.

Another disappointment with the 1841 census for a researcher is that there were very few house names or numbers, especially in a small place like Shalmsford with fewer than 60 households. The lists would not necessarily have been copied into the book in the same order as they appeared in the street, but more likely in the order in which they were collected. This can give some indication as to proximity, such as the households of George and Henry Cork which were recorded sequentially in 1861 and 1871. Of course, all information on the census should be treated with a healthy degree of scepticism. Some false information was given deliberately to deceive, such as parental details, some false information was given, not to deceive but to obscure, for example a person's age, and some was merely an error on the part of the householder or the enumerator.

In 1841, the Shalmsford Street/Bolts Hill area consisted of fifty-seven households, plus The Deanery and Court Lodge Farm.

Shalmsford falls within Enumeration District 2 in Chartham, which comprises 'All that part of the parish of Chartham situated on the south side of the River Stour including Mystole House, Perry Farm, and Little Thruxted in the Denge Woods. (est. 90 houses).' The village of Shalmsford comprises just over half of the dwellings.

The demographic of the village in terms of age changes slightly over time. At the time of the 1841 census there were approximately 70 children under the age of 10 and only three people aged 70-80. Of the under-10s, 10 are less than a year old and another 9 are under 2. As you will see at the end of this section, other evidence shows us that these are only rough numbers and that the numbers recorded on the census are not conclusive

The area is strongly dependent on the land for employment, and there are a few trades shown on the census. I have used the abbreviation 'AL' to denote those engaged as agricultural labourers.

An agricultural labourer earnt about 9 shillings 6 old pence per day, which was, surprisingly, less than they would have earnt had they lived in the northern counties. An average annual wage in Kent was about £25 per year, whereas the average for all counties was £31; a general labourer earnt slightly more, by about 5s per week.

These incomes were supplemented by the work of wives and children, for although a woman had housework to do, and was almost always pregnant or nursing, she also undertook a variety of fieldwork, especially at busy times. In hopping season, the whole family would remove to the hop fields for the day, eating their dinner outside and returning home when the light faded in the evenings. This was piece-work and every hop bine counted.

Occupations in Shalmsford, 1841

| Occupation | No. workers | % working pop. |
|---|---|---|
| Agricultural labourer | 54 | 61% |
| Domestic servant | 9 | 10% |
| Bricklayer | 5 | 6% |
| Blacksmith | 3 | 4% |
| Gardener | 3 | 4% |
| Shoemaker | 3 | 4% |
| Apprentice | 2 | <2% |
| Carpenter | 2 | < 2% |
| Farmer | 2 | <2% |
| Dressmaker | 1 | <1% |
| Grocer | 1 | <1% |
| Mealman | 1 | <1% |
| Publican | 1 | <1% |
| Sawyer | 1 | <1% |
| Total workers | 88 | |

In the evenings, men would work in their cottage garden or allotment, if they were lucky enough to have one. Fresh vegetables were an important part of the diet and if they were not grown, they were bartered for or foraged. Local children were sent out in season to collect the wild harvest of the hedgerows from the tasty new shoots of escapee hops in the spring (those which had set themselves in the hedges, never those from the fields), to baskets of blackberries and plump chestnuts in the autumn, supplementing in between with wild garlic, young nettles and elderflowers. The hop fields and hazel orchards have now gone, but there are still hop vines in the hedgerows along Bobbin Lodge Hill and an abundance of pear, cherry and apple trees by roadsides and in gardens. There is even an ancient walnut tree tucked beside the footpath that runs from Irfon Cottage to the Shalmsford Oast.

he bridge over The River Stour with Shalmsford Bridge Manor in the background

# Trades and Professions

## A Publican at 'The George'

**Jesse Hukins** (40) the publican and his family live at 'The George' public house. Jesse lives with his wife Elizabeth (nee Christian) (34) and their four children Sarah (14), Jesse (10), Philip (6) and Ann (1). Their next child, Lucy, is baptized in September 1842 and the celebrations are no doubt a big family affair involving Jesse's brothers Thomas, below, and Philip, who appears on the next census, along with their families.

The working day was long, as pubs opened around 6am and were not required to close until 11pm, after which there was tidying and restocking work aplenty. The census does not provide us with the occupations of children, but Sarah was more than old enough to be taking a full and active part in the business, cleaning, washing up, and serving in the bar, while son Jesse, at ten years old, would already be a smaller version of his father, moving stock from cellar to bar, sitting in on meetings and amusing the customers with his youthful cheeky comments.

Jesse is renting 'The George' from Messrs Rigden & Delmar. The plot consists of over an acre of house, yard, garden and large pasture behind. Along with 'The George', he rents some arable land on Bolts Hill, behind Box Tree House, and also a house with gardens from Mrs Gellings; looking at the tithe map, I think this may be Walnut Tree Cottage, although I do not know which house he lives in and which he rents out. He also owns an arable field in Chartham and a cottage with garden in Shalmsford Street.

The couple have an older daughter called Elizabeth, who at 16 is visiting elsewhere or has moved away to work as she is not listed on the 1841 census. She moves back home and is shown on the 1851 census, before marrying in 1853. Also living here in the pub are **Charlotte Coleman** (20) a female servant and **John Marsh** (60) who is an odd-job man or caretaker. The servants quarters were usually been tucked up under that rafters, in what is now the loft space, hot in the summer and freezing cold in the winter.

The Chartham parish register of 1849 shows the burial of a woman named Charlotte Christian, aged 49, who I think must have been Jesse's sister-in-law, but I do not know how long she stayed with the family, or whether she had her own house in the area.

The tithe map of 1839 shows that this family live in a house on the northern side of Shalmsford Street opposite what is now described as the Gravel Pit. Jesse owns a small cottage and garden next door, but I think he rents it to another family.

## Three Bricklayers

Jesse's older brother **Thomas Hukins** (50) is a bricklayer and also has a large household. His wife Mary (nee Hall) is 40 and they have five children: Thomas (10), Ambrose (8), named for his grandfather, Charles (6), James (4) and Harriot (6 months). The next child, Frederick is born in March 1844, but dies at 4 months of age. Mary and her sister-in-law Elizabeth, Jesse's wife (above), will be able to support each other as their children grow, sharing tips and stories.

**Charlotte Hall** (14) is also recorded at this address and is a female servant. The Hukins family is large and plays an important part in the life of the village.

**William Philpott** (25), a second bricklayer and his wife Amy (nee Smith) (25) live, with their daughters Sarah (3) and Lydia (1). Bricklayers wore a white or off-white smock until the end of the century, when he favoured overalls instead. The family stay in the area, and although the name of William's wife changes from Amy to Ann on the census, it is the same person, and the fault is in the transcription between census return and enumeration book.

**George Burchett** (60) is the third a bricklayer and he lives with his wife Mary (nee Wood) who is the same age as her husband, in Thruxted Cottage. This house was much more connected to the village before the railway was built. As it is now on its own at the end of a no-through-road and the adjacent land has fallen into disuse, it has become quite isolated.

George and Mary rent rooms in their house to an elderly agricultural labourer, **Edward Bowles** (75), his wife Susannah (75) and their son or grandson Henry

(25), who is also an agricultural labourer. Edward dies before the 1851 census, and Susannah moves to Godmersham to live with her daughter. Henry moves to Canterbury, where he marries and has a large family.

## Three Carpenters

**John Pay,** (AL), and his wife Mary (nee Kibel) are both 65. Their son James (25) is a carpenter. This is the first and only time we see John and Mary, as they both die by the time of the next census. I have been unable to find a record of what happened to James. Their cottage stood on the site of the current houses that comprise numbers 1-5 Shalmsford Street. As the first house in the village, situated conveniently opposite 'The George', Mary was surely one of the first to hear any news brought by carrier and mail coach. If news was expected, she might well have walked to Shalmsford Bridge Cottage, as all traffic had to stop here to pay the road toll – an ideal opportunity to chat to the coachman's mate or horseman.

When at work, John wore a short coat and trousers, a white apron and a square white paper cap to keep the sawdust out of his hair. These caps were worn by many professions, but seem to be mainly associated with carpenters.

Any Victorian village relied on carpenters for furniture, homewares, transport and home repairs, and in a rural location, the skill of the local tradesmen will have been much in demand. **John Martin** (35) is another of the village's carpenters. He lives with his wife Sarah (30) and their children Sarah (12), Alfred (10), and John (3). He is on his was up in the world and by 1861 he lives on Chartham Green and employs one man as well as a boy. Looking at the ages of the children, we see that Sarah gave birth to her daughter when she was 18. In line with tradition, the first girl was named after her mother, and I would expect to see the first boy named after his father, although Alfred may have been named after his grandfather, as a mark of respect. The gap in ages between Alfred and John indicates to me that the couple may have had other children who have died.

**David Handcock** (65) from Wye also works as a carpenter, as does his son William (34) and their live-in apprentice, **James Berwick** (35). David's wife is Susannah (nee Cook) (70) and they live together with David's granddaughter, **Mary Ann Houlden** (20) who might have moved in to help Susannah as she gets older.

The cottage and garden, which they rent, is at the top of Bolts Hill just at the junction with Shalmsford Street, where there is now a row of modern terraced houses. David and Mary Ann move to Canterbury before the next census, and David dies in 1855.

## A Dealer in Meal and Flour

**Harry Gardener** (25) is a mealman, a dealer in meal and flour, who lives in Shalmsford. He will have worked closely with the Corn Mill on what is now the A28 Ashford to Canterbury Road. He lives with his wife Harriatt (nee Hills) who is also 25. Henry had aspirations, and soon moves his family to Maidstone where he is employed as a miller. Henry and Harriatt welcomed their first son, Henry George in February and go on to have five more children.

## Shoe Makers and Menders

Making shoes was an important job and there was plenty of work to go round. There were 4,500 boot and shoemakers recorded in Kent during this decade.

**William Boulder** (35) is one shoemaker, providing essential workwear for the working men of the area. Boots were so important to agricultural workers, that they were one of the first items to be bought with a man's harvest payments in the autumn and despite the hard usage, had to last a year. There are already several shoemakers in the village and William is training **John Stevens** (15), who is recorded as a shoemaker's apprentice. He "lives in", and is looked after by William's wife Sarah (35) along with **Mary Ann Harris** (14) who may be a home help. The tithe map of 1839 records a William Boulding living in Shalmsford Street, whose home was on the south side of the street and was demolished when the railway was cut through.

**Thomas Fox** (64) is another of the village's shoemakers and since his wife (Sophie Burgess from Biddenden) died, he shares his home with **Robert Harris** (50), a labourer and Robert's daughter Eliza (15). **Sarah Gurr** (35) also lives with them, but no details are shown for her occupation or relationship to Mr Fox or Mr Harris. It is interesting to note that the household is still together in 1851, where Sarah is listed as 'housekeeper'. Perhaps the ties are stronger than merely that of housemates.

I think this household was also in the cottages which are now 1-5 Shalmsford Street.

Another little snippet of information gleaned from the parish baptismal records is that a baby called John Gurr who lived in Shalmsford Street was buried in January 1843 aged just 2 months old. There is no reason that this child should be Sarah's, but I think it is a strong possibility.

## Two Farmers

Shalmsford Farm is home to **Thomas Austen** (60) and his wife Sarah (60) with four of their children and their grandson. The oldest son Thomas (30) has taken over management of the farm and gives his occupation as 'farmer' while Thomas Snr no longer works. Although ostensibly retired, I suspect that he still takes the time to give his opinion whether it is asked for or not, while Sarah tries to make him take things easy.

The younger son, Daniel (25), is married to Mary (25), while his sister Elizabeth (20) is still a spinster. As daughter-in-law, Mary has no household of her own to run, and will spend each day negotiating her way through a maze of niceties, having no authority in the house, but still wanting responsibility of her own. She and Daniel have one son, Daniel (2), who will be the focus of her day, as she is torn between maternal instincts and the Victorian mantra of 'spare the rod and spoil the child'.

A closer look at the household reveals that there are no female servants living in, giving an indication that Mary is perhaps expected to fulfil some of the household tasks. Cooking, cleaning, making up fires, preserving food for the winter and working in the dairy would all have been time-consuming, even if Mary's role was only to supervise daily help.

Finch (15) is also Thomas and Sarah's son and he eventually marries Harriet Amos. Finch is a local surname, so could be a reference to a distant relative.

**Thomas Hoare** (35) and **Thomas Ditton** (20) live in the farmhouse in the servants' quarters, in the attic rooms or in a separate outbuilding, and they work as male servants.

This eighteenth-century farm is situated opposite 'The George' public house and has a great deal of associated land. The farm house (now number 7 Shalmsford Street) and the land were rented from Sir John Fagg. Thomas rented his house, garden, barn and yard, plus Marrowbone Field, which he used for arable crops, and pasture land in Two Acres, Drove Lane, Lower, Upper, New Lenty, Greavesfield and Shalmsford fields. Lying beside the River Stour, these fields are rich grazing land. They stretch from the new housing development known as Kingfisher Place to Court Lodge Farm and are still used as grazing for sheep.

Thomas Austin Snr dies in 1849, and a notice of sale in the local newspaper tells us that the farm is to be sold. The sale includes six useful draught horses, two milch cows, one heifer, five store hogs, wagons, carts, ploughs, harrows, rolls, nidget, etc . Also, brewing and dairy utensils. Sale to commence at 11 o'clock with the household furniture.

The milk from the cows and the bacon from the pigs was no more than was needed for the family, but it is possible that some surplus was available for sale in times of plenty. This was mainly an arable farm.

The second farm in Shalmsford village is Court Lodge Farm at the opposite end of the village from Shalmsford Farm, which is occupied by **Thomas Gambrill** (39) with his wife Elizabeth (30), his brother Austen (20) and their children Austen (2), Thomas (1) and Ann (4). The family live in a state of relative luxury, with a large house and an income derived from the farm. This can be seen by the number of servants they employ. The couple married late in life, being 35 and 25 respectively, in 1837, which could reflect the fact that they held some wealth and needed to make an appropriate match rather than a love match.

There are five live-in servants, **Phoebe Cobb** (15), whose parents live in the village, **Stephen Spillett** (25), **James Cole** (25), **Thomas Waller** (15) and **William Baldock** (15). Although these people live on-site, I do not know their exact occupations. I assume Phoebe is a domestic servant and the men work on the farm. How lucky she was to have benefited from the occasional gift of less fashionable but still good quality clothing from her mistress.

A Family of Bricklayers

The Adams family home is number 42 Shalmsford Street, on the corner of Shalmsford Street and Thruxted Lane, which was built in the mid-eighteenth-century and is still known as Adams Cottage. **Frances Adams** (nee Fox) (60) is the matriarch of a household of seven, since the death of her husband Robert Tritton Adams ten years earlier. She lives on independent means and owns her own home, which she shares with her two children, her daughter Frances (25), a dressmaker, and her son John (40). Also in the house are John's wife Mary (40) and their children Harriot (14), John (17) and Tritton (15).

The work undertaken by daughter Frances was time-consuming and complex, as clothing was all hand-sewn at this time. It was not until later in the century that treadle sewing machines, operated by the foot of the seamstress, were available to home-workers. The hours of work would still be long, but the operator could at least sit upright instead of bent over her work, compressing her vital organs and straining her eyes.

John and his sons all work as bricklayer's labourers. This was an age when a man's profession was recognised by his dress and they would each have worn a labourer's jacket of white flannel, white stockings, brogues and a low, round, flat cap.

Harriot marries John Norton of Bridge before the next census, and it is sad to note burial records for two of Harriot's children, one for Harriot Jane Norton on October 26th 1850, when she was just 23, and another for John Joseph Adams in 1843, when he is aged 19.

## The Village Shop

Opposite the Adams' is **Phineas Shrubsole** (45) who is a grocer by trade, but who also owns some land in the area. He lives with his wife Ester (nee Denton), who is from the Isle of Wight, but they currently have no children. They share the dwelling with **George Penn** (30), a male servant, and **Phoebe Burch** (35), a female servant. These are shown on the census living at the same address, but in a separate household, so the house might be divided. However, it seems more likely that they were employed by Mr Shrubsole in the grocer's shop and 'lived in', making do with draughty servants' quarters high in the loft space of the house.

The Shrubsoles own their own property, which is now number 42 Shalmsford Street, as well as others in the village, including the houses they rent to Thomas Baldock, William Newton and others. The home in which they live is a generously-sized house with a yard, buildings, garden, home orchard and pasture.

Adams Cottage

One of the items in stock was no doubt commercial soap, although at roughly the same cost as a joint of beef, its use was beyond the means of most of the Shalmsford inhabitants. Their cleansing routine was more likely to have been a good rub down with a dry linen cloth, possibly followed by a quick sprinkle of talcum powder, as described by Ruth Goodman in her book 'How to be a Victorian'.

## One Sawyer

The next professional in Shalmsford Street is **Charles Cook** (55) who is a sawyer and lives with two women called Mary, one who is fifty and one who is sixty. He married Mary Farbrace in 1809 and it is reasonable to assume that the other woman is his unmarried sister. I wonder if the sisters-in-law adopted nick-names to help them retain their separate identities.

## Two Gardeners

Living in Bolts Hill is **John Gould** (65), a gardener, who lives with his wife Sarah (60) and his son Henry (20), who works as an agricultural labourer. John dies later this year, although Sarah goes on to live another twenty years. The term 'gardener' refers to someone who undertakes market gardening as well as one who tends the flower beds. The tithe map shows that he rented a house and garden plus another garden, which I take to mean market garden, not flower garden.

**James Stubberfield** (55) is another gardener, this time at Court Lodge at the bottom of the hill and he almost certainly lives in the gardener's cottage on site. It would be easy to identify his occupation as his apron would be of blue cloth, which he wore to distinguish himself from other labourers who worked on the land; Victorian gardeners were considered to be a step above other workers. He lives with his wife Ann (nee Crotholl) (55) and his son Joseph (25) who works with him as a gardener. This family also continues in the area for many generations.

In future census returns, we see the Court Lodge gardener living in Rose Cottage, now on the opposite side of the railway to Court Lodge Farm, and much enlarged. This could well be the home of James Stubberfield and his family in 1841.

The 1842 tithe map shows James Stupperfield renting a substantial amount of land from John Wraith, which tells us that he was in receipt of a generous wage. The properties concerned are a house & premises, stable & yard, garden, osier ground & pasture and a slip. These tracts of land are all around the Deanery Oast area, opposite the current Chartham Surgery buildings. Osiers are a relative of the willow family and are coppiced on wet land to produce thin, flexible rods suitable for basket weaving. These would need to be stripped of their outer layer of bark before they could be used, hence the name of the popular country dance 'Strip the Willow'.

The other people in the village who undertake identifyable trades and professions are all sons or daughters living at home, so I have listed them with their families.

## Agricultural Labourers

These are families where the head of the household has identified himself as an agricultural labourer (AL). Wives and children were also earning a small income, but this is not always noted. It is also interesting to see that many of the older children are working, some in recognised trades of higher social status than their parents.

I have divided the inhabitants into those who live in Shalmsford Street and those who live in the Bolts Hill area, purely because this information was recorded on the census. I have no way of knowing which house belongs to which family.

## Shalmsford Street

Most of the men who live in Shalmsford work as agricultural labourers. This includes a wide range of occupations on the farm, in the fields and in woodland areas. These men are immensely fit, walking up to six miles a day to get to and from their place of work before undertaking 9-10 hours of physically demanding activity. We should also remember that there were few Bank Holidays and that Sunday was the only day of rest during the week.

Their wives keep house, make the family's clothes, cook and take on ad hoc jobs in the neighbourhood such as seasonal field work. Also, many of the children listed here will undertake field work from a very young age, although this is not reflected in the list of occupations. Even the very young ones carried out jobs like taking beer or 'bait' (food) to their fathers in the fields at lunchtime.

One of the many disadvantages of agricultural labour was that it was seasonal, so a man had to have a range of skills, and that the tasks were dependent upon the weather. If the weather was bad a man was sent home without pay. This was particularly hard in villages such as Shalmsford where such a large proportion of the population depended on this work.

An agricultural labourer wears clothes of undyed cotton or wool, in as many layers as could be achieved. During the winter months, when extra layers were unobtainable, newspapers and other papers were used as insulation against the biting winds. Over their vests, shirts, waistcoat and jacket, some of the older men wear smocks, again made from undyed cotton, cut in a square fashion and pleated to give shape.

A man's trousers were made from canvas twill or a heavy fabric known as 'jean', from which we get the modern term for trousers made from denim. A pair of gaiters tied around the lower leg added protection and warmth, even when they were as simple as a piece of sacking tied on with string.

For protection against sun and rain, a round-crowned soft hat made of felted wool is the favoured item. This may have become baggy and mis-shapen over the years, but a favourite hat does much to give comfort to a man of meagre means.

## A Small Family

I start with **Joseph Washford** (50) (AL) who lives with his wife Sarah (nee Bristow) (45) and their children Harriot (15) and Sarah (10).

There is a burial record for Sarah Washford, who dies aged 21 in October 1847. This could be the Washford's daughter, as the ages recorded on documents are seldom accurate.

## A Family of Daughters

**Thomas Cobb** (AL) is 45 and his wife Sally (nee Uden), also 45, live with the youngest of their children, Sarah (11) and Emily (9). They had five older daughters, one of whom died in infancy; the other four have left home. Their daughter Phoebe is still in the area and works at Court Lodge, situated between the hamlet of Shalmsford and Chartham Village proper. This family do not appear on the 1851 census, but in 1861 are found living in Faversham. Although Phoebe is living so near to them, they would only have seen her once a week, on a Sunday, as she lived at the farm.

## A Full House

It is a very different story at the home of **William Ward** (45) (AL) and his wife Sarah (40) who still have six of their children at home: Charlotte (20), George (16) (also an agricultural labourer), Elender (or Eleanor) (14), Charles (11), Thomas (5) and Alfred (2). Having this number of children at home can make the house noisy and crowded, but the couple are obviously happy with this as they would otherwise have encouraged the older children to leave home. This household is one of the more affluent of the agricultural labourers' homes as all but the youngest two bringing in a wage. I can find no mention of any one of this family after their appearance on this census, and it is possible that they emigrated.

William and his family live at the corner of Bolts Hill and Shalmsford Street on what is now a new development, next door to David Handcock the carpenter.

## A Step-mother for Mary

**William Baker** (40), (AL), and his wife Eliza (nee Marsh) (30) live with Mary (14), Charlotte (4) and Eliza (1). William and Eliza have been married since 1832, and Mary is William's child from a previous marriage. Following the death of his first wife he married Eliza, and Charlotte and Eliza are their children, which explain why they are so much younger than Mary. We can follow William's life as we look at the census returns for the coming decades. Their daughter Jane is born in 1848.

## The Sad Reality of Infant Mortality

**George Cork** (20) (AL) is married to his first wife Mary (25) and they live with their daughters Charlotte (4) and Sarah (9 months). His father Thomas is round the corner in Shalmsford Street. The Cork family is a large one, and we will be seeing a lot more of them as we unravel the information provided by the census.

The church records show a child called George being baptized on July 14th 1844. His parents are given as George and Elizabeth Cork with the address of Shalmsford Street. Given the confusion over Mary and Elizabeth (see 1851 census), I still think this is the right family. However, the baby dies at 9 weeks.

Another child, Henry Cork, is registered in May 1847 but dies in 1851.

Lastly, I found a baptism record for William in August 1849, for whom I do not see a death record.

## Keeping Close

**Thomas Cork**, (AL), and his wife Sarah (nee Bass) are both 60 and have been married since 1805. The two girls in the house are Sarah (20) and Frances (15) who are their two oldest daughters. Their son George lives in Shalmsford Street with his family, while three other sons and their daughter Jane have moved away. On the next census, we see them living with their son Henry and his family.

## A Close-knit Family

**James Link** (35) (AL) and his wife Jane (nee Partis) (30) have five children: James (12), Ann (11), John (5), Sarah (3) and Maria (6 months). Ann was undoubtedly required to look after their younger brothers and sisters and to help with the housework while her mother dealt with the new baby. James is brother to William Link who lives nearby with his wife Hannah, and son to William and Maria.

It is likely that poor, overworked Jane, used the country practise of raising her babies without nappies before they could crawl. The lack of running water made the constant washing of nappies impossible, so babies were laid directly onto an absorbent mattress of hay or straw, which kept them dry. A layer of lard smeared onto the baby's bottom helped keep nappy rash at bay.

Jane gave birth to George in 1848.

## Glad to be near the Grandchildren

William Link (65) (AL) and Maria (68) have no children at home, but their sons James and William live in Shalmsford Street and they see them regularly.

## Another Large Family

James' brother, **William Link** (40) (AL) lives with his wife Hannah (nee Taylor) (35) and their children William (14), Charlotte (12), John (10), Henry (8), Maria (6), James (3). Another child with the same surname, Mary (10) is also shown at this address who is probably a cousin, staying with the family. The children in this family are of a similar age to their cousins, James and Jane's children, and, given half a chance, would no doubt have sneaked off together after church on Sunday.

William and Hannah have two more children while living in Shalmsford Street. Rachel is baptized on January 15th 1843, and Edward on December 14th 1845, but by 1851 they have moved into Mill Cottage in Chartham and have nine children at home. William's parents also live in Shalmsford Street.

## Extended Family Welcome

Next is the home of **Thomas Homersham** (50) (AL) and his wife Charlotte (nee Drury) (55) with their children James (9), Charles (6), Mercy (5) and Charlotte (3). Also in the house is Esther Homersham (15), Thomas' niece, and daughter of his brother William. **Frances Knight** (7) is staying with the family, and is almost certainly a grandchild.

## Double Trouble

**William Hayward** (50) (AL) lives with his wife Thomazin (nee Tucker) (45) and his daughter Harriot (25). The twins **James and John Urquehart** (13) are also recorded at this address, but I have not been able to find a link between them and the Haywards; they are perhaps relatives who have come to stay, either temporarily or on a permanent basis, or they could be foster children. William and Thomazin continue to live in Shalmsford Street, although the boys and Harriot move away.

## A Single Man

**Ralph Fox** is 74 and lives on independent means, either inherited or saved money or a pension.

## Living at 'Loam Pits'

**George Burchett,** (AL) and his wife Ann are both recorded as being 50. However, a closer look at the original document shows that 54 has been entered and then altered to show the rounded down figure of 50. They live with Thomas (20) and Henry (15) both agricultural labourers, plus Ester (13) and Susannah (1).

Ann dies two years later, with the address given as 'Loam Pits' and is buried on 25th January 1843. The tithe map of 1839 shows the name Loam Pits associated with gardens near Thruxted Cottage, although at this time the land is rented to 'Mr Wackford and others.' This address has been divided from Thruxted Cottage by the railway line, and is now used as pasture for horses and ponies. It is located by the entrance to Chilham Lakes.

Records show that Henry and Elizabeth Burchett who live in Shalmsford Street welcome a son, William, into their family in 1850. This must be George Snr's grandchild.

## George's Sons Stay Nearby

George's son **Philip Burchett** (25) (AL) has two children and he and his wife Maryann (nee Gibson) (26) ; Maryann (2) and Philip (4 months). By 1851 this family has moved out of Shalmsford Street and are living in Boughton Aluph.

Philip's brother, **George Burchett** (30), lives with his wife Mary (nee Marsh) (31).

It could be this couple who are the parents of George Tritton Burchett, born in 1844, son of George and Mary Burchett who live in Shalmsford Street. The father's occupation is given as shoemaker, so this rules out 'The George' Burchetts who are bricklayers, but it is hard to sort them out. Sadly, young George Tritton dies aged six months. It is interesting to wonder why this child is called Tritton when the other Trittons in the village all have the surname Adams.

## Baptizing the Twins

**William Loram,** (AL) and his wife Elizabeth (nee Arbin) are both 35. They were married in 1830 and now have seven children, Mary (10), George (9), Jesse and Charles who are both 8, William (5), Eliza (3) and Michael (1). Elizabeth is the only person in Shalmsford Street who was born in a different village. Their oldest daughter Mary eventually marries twice, but stays in the village both times.

It is interesting to note that even though Jesse and Charles are both recorded as eight years old on the 1841 census, the Chartham baptism records show that Charles was baptised in March 1833 and Jesse was baptised in June 1833. One would think that if they boys were twins, they almost certainly have been baptised at the same time and might question the information given.

Luckily, the issue is resolved when the original baptism record is consulted. Despite the fact that the boys have different dates of baptism, they are clearly marked with the word 'twins' in the margin. It was not uncommon that a family could not afford to have both children baptised at the same time, and that the weaker child was baptised first.

One final point to mention about this family is that they are soon to lose their youngest member; Michael dies when he is five, in 1844.

## A Family of Ten

**George Hoare**, (AL) is the same age as his wife, Mary (nee Back); they are both 35. Having been married since 1826, George may be happy to leave the house full of children in the morning, while Mary looks after James (13), Phoebe (11), Maryann (9), Sophia (7), Harriott (5), Ellen (3), George (2) and baby Sarah who is just six months old. Little do they know that they will be joined by three more before the time of the next census. The first of these will be Jesse who is baptized in November 1842, followed by Emma in 1846 and lastly John in 1847, who dies the same year.

George is son to Richard and Phoebe and when the children escaped from the house to play, preferring the bright, spacious outdoors and relishing the lack of parental oversight, they will have made it a priority to visit their grandparents in search of a treat or two.

Richard Hoare, (AL), and his wife Phoebe (nee Benton) are both 60. Phoebe dies a year after the census was taken in the winter of 1842, and Richard moves in with his youngest daughter, Eliza.

The tithe map shows that Richard rents a piece of land which he uses as pasture. The plot is a small island in the middle of The River Stour, so was very convenient for keeping animals from wandering free. The term 'pasture' implies cows, but he might just as easily be keeping sheep or pigs.

## No Retirement for William

William Warden (AL) is 70 but still working, for we must not forget there were no old age pensions in 1841. He lives with his wife Mary (nee Curtis) (60) and son Richard (25) (AL). His son John is husband to Jane Warden, making Mary, Julia, George and Frances Warden their grandchildren. Richard eventually marries and moved to Chartham Village and by 1861 he and his wife have ten children.

William dies in 1848 and is buried on May 23rd, but Mary lives a long life in Shalmsford Street.

## Her Maiden Name is not Forgotten

The household of William Newton (30) lies between that of Jesse Hukins and

James Foster. They rent their home One of the few entries with an address is that of William Cozens, who lives at 'Barnes'. This refers to the eighteenth century houses known as Barn Cottages, which are now numbers 14, 16 & 18 Shalmsford Street. William (55), (AL), lives with his wife Sarah.) (57) and their sons William (28) (AL), and Edward (18), a blacksmith. The family stay in the area, moving to a house in Bolts Hill later in the decade.

## An Age of Male Superiority

John Pay (40) (AL) has recorded his family by gender, with the males being listed before the females. His wife, Elizabeth (nee Philpott) (40) and he were married in 1825 and they now have five children at home: Nicholas (14), Maria (9), John (5), Catherine (3) and James, 10 months. John and his family continue to live in Chartham and John finds employment on the railway when it arrives.

John and Elizabeth have another baby in the summer of 1843, called Edwin, who dies six months later, and I have also found the burial record of an Elizabeth Pay, aged 45, who I believe to be John's wife. She was buried in February 1843.

## Premature Death was a Fact of Life

**Thomas Leeds** (60) (AL) lives with his wife Mary or May (nee Izzard Reader) (55). Their son Thomas Leeds (35), who also works as an agricultural labourer, still lives in the house with his family along with his sisters Susan (18), Catherine (15) and Jane (11). The couple's unmarried daughter Elizabeth (30) looks after her sons William Leeds (6) and Jesse Coleman Leeds who is 10 months old. Thomas dies in 1844, and Mary, Thomas Jnr and Jane move to Nickel Cottages, just to the north-east of the village.

This family has a great deal of heartache to come, as the eldest son John dies in 1843, aged 27, just before his father, and Susan is listed in the parish burial records in February 1846, when she dies aged 24.

## A Family of Unmarried Mothers

**Elizabeth Vincer** (nee Cobb) (50) lives with her daughters Elizabeth (30), Mary (15) and her grandson Charles Ruck Vincer (10). Charles is Elizabeth's son.

Elizabeth's daughter Frances (25) has married **Joseph Spillett** (20), (AL), and they live in the same household, with their daughter Eliza (1). Joseph Spillett dies in 1847 and is buried on September 14th after which Frances continues to live with her mother. The address of the family at this time is Box Trees.

This family is rather confusing due to duplicate names and several unmarried mothers. I have included a family tree as an appendix to show my thoughts on the matter. This family has a long history in the village and continues to intrigue me.

The parish records include a record of the baptism of a boy called Stephen in 1843, with Maria, a spinster of Shalmsford Street being shown as his mother, although there is also a record of the death of a Stephen Vincer in this same year, which I assume is this baby.

**James Smith** (58), (AL), lives with his wife Sarah (55). If they had children, they have all left home now. The cottage and garden are rented from Edward Denne but by 1851, Sarah is recorded as a pauper in Bridge, Kent.

## Brother and Sister

**Sarah Spickett** (35) is a widow who lives with her daughter Eliza (10) and shares with her brother John Marsh (20), an agricultural labourer. She married Edward Spickett in 1829, in Chartham church, but he died in 1833. Both Edward and Sarah made their marks on the marriage register alongside that of William Spickett, Edward's father, rather than signing their names.

It is surprising to find a record in the Chartham parish records of a baptism in 1843, ten years after Edward's death. The child's name is Sarah, and the mother is Sarah Spickett, widow, of Shalmsford Street. The couple move away before the next census, but return to the village when Sarah Snr is older.

## A Strong Woman

The husband of **Jane Warden** (nee Gibson) is away from home. She is only 25 and looks after her children Mary (5), Julia (4), George (2) and Frances (4 months). When her husband dies in 1846 she remarries, choosing Henry Wright. After their marriage in 1850 they move out of the village.

It is sad to note that baby Frances also dies. A record in the parish register shows a burial date of April 15 1842, when she was 15 months old.

Barnes Cottages

## Keeping her Sons Close

The household of **Ann Young** (60) contains her sons John (20) and William (15), both agricultural labourers. I have been unable to decipher her occupation. By 1851 John has found employment as a servant.

## Two Homes in One, Plus Lodgers!

**John Hulse** (60) is an agricultural labourer and shares his home with his wife, Ann, who is the same age. The house holds another family, the Hukins, consisting of **Philip Hukins** (48) a bricklayer, his wife Catherine (nee Edmonds) (45) and their son William (3). **Frederick Edmans** (6) and **James Hall** (45) are also recorded at the same address. It is likely that Frederick is a relative and James is a lodger.

## A Fledgling Family

**Charles and Emma Warden** are both twenty and have only been married a year. Charles works as an agricultural labourer, and Emma will be looking forward to the birth of her baby or hoping to become pregnant in the near future. By the next census return, they have four children, the first, William, arriving in July 1843, and their second, James in 1845.

Perhaps Charles is brother-in-law to Jane warden, also in the village, and helps her out while his brother is away.

## More Twins in the Village

**John Barker** (40), (AL), and Mary (nee Lade) (30) already have a large family at home. Their oldest son Joseph (13) was followed by twins Edward and Mary (10), Charles (7), Ann (4) and Elizabeth (1). This family continues to live and grow in the area for many generations.

# Bolts Hill

Turning into Bolts Hill, but still within the hamlet of Shalmsford, we find **Henry Mutton** (40) (AL), and his wife Sarah (nee Waller) (35). Their son Robert (15) is still at home, and works as an agricultural labourer. The family soon move away to live in Dover.

## Box Trees House

Box Trees House is set back from the road and has a view over Chartham village; it is said to date from the fifteenth century. It is home to **Sarah Pay** (60), her daughter or daughter-in-law Mary (20) and her grandchildren Ann (5) and Emily (1). The family stay in the area for many years.

## Box Tree Cottages

The residence recorded as 'Boxtrees' refers to Box Tree Cottages, now a pair of listed cottages at the bottom on the hill, and is home to the following five families:

**William Philpott** (30) (AL) and his wife Harriot (nee Marsh) (25) have three children: John (3), Mary (1) and baby Sarah (2 months). William and Harriot move to Shalmsford Street as their family grow.

There is a baptism record for George Philpott, whose parents are William and Harriet at the same address in August 1842, which shows that their family grows quickly before they move towards the end of the decade.

**John Philpott** (60) (AL) lives with his wife Sarah (50) and their children John (18) (AL) and Eliza (15). Eliza later marries James Frier but continues to live in Bolts Hill. I cannot find a concrete connection between William and John, but I assume they are related.

**Thomas Gipson** (50) (AL) lives with Mary (50) and their son William (12). The Gipson family thrive and continue to live in the area for many years. The Canterbury Archives show a receipt to Thomas Gipson for transporting 15 loads of stones at 6d a load from Chartham to Canterbury in 1841. Although this Thomas works mainly as an agricultural labourer, he undertook other work as it presented itself. Given the fact that the family business is soon that of carriers and coal carters, it is very likely that this is the same man.

Thomas's brother, **Richard Gipson** (AL) (45) and his wife Elizabeth (nee Cudham) (45) live on their own.

**Robert Laker** (25) (AL) lives with his wife Jane (nee Couter) (30) and **Mary Gipson** (50). Robert's mother was Sarah Gratnell, which makes him nephew to Elizabeth Gipson who lives next door.

Having reviewed the census information, I think Mary Gipson has been recorded twice, once in this household, where she actually stayed on the night, and with her husband Thomas, where she usually lives. There seems to be no reason for her to stay at the Lakers' house overnight, when she only lives a few doors away, unless Robert or Jane was ill. It is possible that Jane was in labour that night, and Mary was assisting.

By 1851, Robert has moved to Harbledown to live with his brother, and I cannot find Jane, so I assume she has died.

## Other records

The census is a great snapshot of the village on that particular night, but people are born, die and move about fairly regularly, and not everyone is included. A lot can happen in the ten years between and the records can be misleading.

Unless another address is specifically mentioned, all the children listed below were born in Shalmsford Street.

- The registers mention Stephen and Caroline Spillett. They are on the church records as the parents of Martha, baptized 24th March 1844, Hester, baptized 14th December 1845, Eliza, who is baptized on 6th February 1848 and Martha, baptized 4th November 1849. The first Martha and Eliza both die in 1848. This couple appear on the 1851 census, so must have moved into the area just after 1841. Alternatively, this could be the Stephen Spillett who works at Court Lodge, and his wife who was missed from the census.

- Another birth is that of Richard, to Richard and Sarah Warden in 1845. Richard is a labourer, and this is his first child, as the boy carries his name.

- James Samuel Wright and his wife Susannah Elizabeth also have a child in 1845. Thomas Edward is baptized on 23rd February 1845.

- George and Charlotte Spillett baptized their son George on March 9th 1845.

- Yet another young couple are William and Frances Young, whose daughter Sarah Ann is baptised in February 2846.

- John and Mary Appleton are also missing from the census information. They welcome their daughter Hannah in the spring of 1846 and she is baptized on 3rd May at the same time as John and Mary Baker's son John.

- A baby boy, George Stanner Stevens, was born to Mary Ann Austen, spinster in 1842. His father is John Stanner Stevens Austen.

- Eliza joins the family of Richard and Elise Linkin in January 1843.

- Another baby is born into the Linkin family in the same year, this time to Henry and Sarah. Lydia is baptised on 12th March.

- A son, Thomas, is born to Thomas and Mary Ann Cork.

- Mary Ann Knight was born to Susannah and James Samuel Ham Knight in 1848, but they move to Harbledown.

- Edward is born to Rebecca Fowles, widow in 1848. I assume it is a posthumous son of her husband, but Edward could be a love child.

- Henry and Jane Cork, who we see on subsequent census returns, are already living in the area in 1848, when their son Henry is born, but he dies in 1851.

- Baby Edward is born to James and Elizabeth Austin in 1849.

- As with the births, some people moved into the village only shortly before their death and so their details do not appear on the census records. The death records I have found are:

- Mary Ann Maple, who was buried in St Mary's churchyard on 4th August 1850, aged 37. Her address is recorded as being in Shalmsford Street.

- Mary Cork who was buried 30th November 1842, aged 64.

- Frances Hoare is born in 1843 but dies aged 3 months and is buried in October. Her parents are Richard and Elizabeth Hoare of Shalmsford Street. Richard is son to Richard and Phoebe and brother to George. I have also found the baptism record for twins Ann and Harriet Hoare, with the same parents, in January 1848. Harriet dies aged 8 months, but Ann lives.

- Another child to die in Shalmsford Street in this decade is Mary Ann Wood, who was buried 16th December 1847. She was the daughter of George and Louisa Wood.

- It is always sad to see the death of a child, and even more poignant when the parents cannot be identified. Little Ann oare of Shalmsford Street died in1847 at 3 months, but I cannot find her family. I hope her parents aren't Richard and Elizabeth, as above.

- Phebe Spillett was buried on 22nd April 1848, aged 19. She was niece to both Stephen and Caroline Spillett and Joseph and Frances, being the daughter of their brother Thomas

# The 1850s

Kent has seen some bad weather since the last census, with violent thunderstorms and hail in 1846, heavy rain in the winter of 1846/7 and a snowstorm which covered south eastern England in 1849. The autumn of 1850, just before the census had also been windy, with an October gale so strong that the packet steamer RMS Royal Adelaide had run aground in Margate with the loss of all 250 crew and passengers. Despite the distance from sleepy Chartham, news of this disaster no doubt reached the village quite quickly.

An Act of Parliament was passed in 1857 which required every borough and county to set up a local police force. Up until this date the local police officer interpreted the law according to the ideas of the local landowners/magistrates. As travel between towns and villages become increasingly easy, so crime increased, and more constables were needed. It was recognised that at first these would be largely illiterate, although officers had to be able to read and write. After three months training at Maidstone, constables were issued with a pocket guide and a uniform and put to work.

The average weekly wage for an agricultural labourer at this time was about 9 shillings and sixpence a week, based on a 10 ½ hour day. They had risen by only 1s in the past twenty years, and times were hard.

The railway line from Ashford to Canterbury has now been completed, but the people of Chartham initially voted not to have a station in their village, although one was opened at Chilham in 1846. Anyone with the time and money to spare could easily have walked there to catch a train, and I wonder if anyone from the village visited The Great Exhibition in 1851. They would certainly have read about it in the newspapers of the time.

One snippet of news in the Maidstone and South Eastern Gazette dated Sept 9th 1851 will have caused the local people who voted against the railway a moment of quiet satisfaction, when Edward Brett of Canterbury met with an accident on the railway line at Shalmsford Street.

'He was about the jump onto one of the trucks of a ballast train to skid it when he missed his footing, one of his feet lodging on the line, and before he could have time to remove it the wheel of an empty truck passed over and dislocated the great toe.'

The poor man was taken to Kent and Canterbury Hospital, but nay-sayers may have seen this as a vindication of their choice to have nothing to do with the railway.

People were more alarmed by the reports of an accident in August 1858, when a train derailed near Chilham, killing three people and injuring 16.

# The 1851 Census

The 1851 census counted those in residence on the night of 30th March. The 1841 census has been taken in June, and enumerators had found that many families were too busy with the early harvest to be overly concerned about filling in forms and returning them on the correct day.

Enumeration District 2 now comprises 'All that part of the Parish of Chartham situated on the south side of the River Stour including Perry Farm, Thruxted Farm, Underdown cottages, Mystole House, Pickleden, Shalmsford Street, Bolts Hill, Chartham Deanery and Court Lodge Farm, Radigund Street and Horton Chapel Farm.'

There are now 68 households in the Shalmsford Street/Bolts Hill area, and it is interesting to see that only five men have reached the required level of property ownership to merit inclusion on the Electoral Register: Thomas Newington, Phineas Shrubsole Jnr, Thomas Hukins, Jesse Hukins and Philip Hukins.

The demographic in terms of age has changed slightly. There are now approximately the same number of children under the age of 10 (75), with the proviso that the census figures are not entirely accurate, but there are significantly more older people. The number of 70-80 year olds has risen from 3 to 12.

For the purposes of this census, enumerators were required to enter the occupation of the wife the same as that of the husband, which further muddies the waters of accuracy.

This has led to some misleading information. However, many of the people in Shalmsford Street are agricultural labourers and working class and of the wives do indeed have worked as agricultural labourers either alongside their husbands or in alternative industries. It is also often the case that an older child are left to look after the children while the mother works, as a woman's wages, albeit lower than a man's, are still higher than that of a child, even a boy. After much deliberation, I have left out the occupation of the wives in this census unless I have found additional evidence.

The people in the village vary very little from those who lived here in 1841, but it is possible to see the beginning of an influx of new blood. It is in this second, more detailed, census that we also begin to see the level of intermarriage between the various families.

Another difference in this census is that we now see several of the tradesman labelled as 'journeymen'. A tradesman needed to be apprenticed in order to learn his trade, and I have found several apprenticed living in Shalmsford Street in this census. The journeymen are the qualified tradesmen, who have completed their apprenticeships.

You will note that few children are listed as scholars. This is because the cost of schooling was prohibitive to most, and the income from a child labourer made all the difference between survival and otherwise to a poor family. However, it is encouraging to see that three-quarters of children attend Sunday School, although fewer than 40% of the population were regular church-goers. This was a full-time day of schooling, paid for by the church, which covered the 'three Rs', reading, writing and arithmetic.

Children were offered a smallpox vaccine from 1854, which was the start of world eradication of the disease, finally achieved in 1980.

## Trades and Professions

As more people become involved in distinct trades, I have followed the lead of the enumerator and divided the information into two sections, for Shalmsford Street and for Bolts Hill. In reality, these were just two parts of the same village.

Occupations in Shalmsford, 1851

| Agricultural labourer | 47 | 47% |
|---|---|---|
| Carpenter | 8 | 8% |
| Bricklayer | 5 | 5% |
| Dressmaker/Seamstress | 4 | 4% |
| Domestic servant | 3 | 3% |
| Paper mill | 3 | 3% |
| Plumber | 3 | 3% |
| Sawyer | 3 | 3% |
| Shoemaker | 3 | 3% |
| Carrier | 2 | 2% |
| Farmer | 2 | 2% |
| Gardener | 2 | 2% |
| Grocer | 2 | 2% |
| Railway labourer | 2 | 2% |
| Teacher | 2 | 2% |
| Baker | 1 | 1% |
| Blacksmith | 1 | 1% |
| Housekeeper | 1 | 1% |
| Licenced victualler | 1 | 1% |
| Nurse | 1 | 1% |
| Railway Gate Keeper | 1 | 1% |
| Wheelwright | 1 | 1% |
| Woodsman | 1 | 1% |
|  |  |  |
|  | 99 |  |

# Shalmsford Street

## The Railway Brings Employment

**Francis Somerford** (57) is a Railway Gate Keeper who lives with his wife Sarah (50) and their sons Richard (11) and George (9). It is interesting to note that people are now becoming more mobile in search of employment, following a calling or profession rather than working the land near their place of birth. Francis was born in Brenchley and his wife was born in Sturry, a village just north of Canterbury. His sons were both born in Fordwich, near Sturry, on the other side of Canterbury.

The nearest level crossing to Shalmsford Street is the one on Thruxted Lane, where there was a small house similar to the one illustrated. Francis continues to work on the railway, but is soon moved up the line to work nearer to Ashford. He opens the gates manually when vehicles want to cross, maintains the lights on the gates and possibly operates the signals as well.

## A Village Blacksmith

Again we meet **Thomas Homersham** (65) (AL) from Canterbury, who lives with his wife Charlotte (62). They share their house with their son James (20) a journeyman blacksmith and their daughter Charlotte (13). Although their children Charles and Mercy have now left home. Thomas is beginning to slow down now, but he stays in Shalmsford Street and is retired by 1861.

When at work, Thomas wore ankle-length thick leather apron split down the front to protect him from the heat and yet still allow him to move with ease. He would also have been the farrier, shoeing work horses. The family may have lived at number 21 Shalmsford Street, which is known as The Old Forge.

## Four Carpenters

These carpenters have taken over from John Pay and David Handcock, who have now passed away. There is more than enough work in the village for all of them.

A new face in Shalmsford Street is **Thomas Ford** (27) from Canterbury, who has married Chilham girl Ann (nee Harlow) (31); their first child Ann is just four months old. Thomas works as a carpenter and joiner, but it seems the work is not to his liking as he soon moves back to Canterbury where he takes a job as a grocer.

Next is another new family: **William Harvey** (24), a carpenter from Waltham, and his family. His wife Ester (23) was born in Sturry and their children are Marshall (2) and Stephen (2 months). A daughter, Lucy, is born in 1853. We do not see this family again, although I know that they do have two more children: Mark, in 1854 and Ann in 1856, before they move.

**Charles Ruck** (36) is also new to the village since the 1841 census, when he lived in Rattington Street in Chartham. Charles works is a journeyman carpenter and lives with his wife Matilda (nee Long) (35). Their children are William (11), Agnes (5) and Hannah (9 months). This family stay in the area and continue to provide service to the community as qualified carpenters.

There is a parish burial record for a child called Charles Henry Ruck dated 21st April 1846, who was Charles and Matilda's son.

It is also sad to note that their son Walter Bligh Ruck, who was baptized on August 27th 1855, died seven months later in early 1856.

Charles was awarded 15s at the 1859 Annual Ploughing Match for his service to Mr Foreman.

**James Pay** (40) is the last journeyman carpenter to be listed. He lives with his wife Ann (39) who is from Sellindge, near Ashford, and their children Susannah (5), Benjamin Norris (3) and Sarah (1 month).

**Jesse Hukins** (50), who gave his occupation as 'publican' on the last census is now a carpenter employing eight other men. He lives with his wife Elizabeth (45) from Petham and their children. The two oldest boys Jesse (18) and Philip (15) are old enough to work and are employed by their father as carpenters. The next boy, William is thirteen and is still a scholar, as are Mary Jane (7) and Frederick (4). The oldest son, Jesse Jnr. goes on to be an architect and surveyor.

Jesse and Elizabeth's next child is Edward, born in 1854 and I have found a burial record for Edward Hukins in 1858, which may be for this child.

Jesse owns enough property to be listed on the Electoral Register, although it is interesting to note that on the register of 1852 his address is given as Shalmsford Street, so he must have moved soon after the census.

## A Publican at 'The George'

Next is an establishment, run by 'Licensed Victualler' **Edward Keeler** (31), who was licenced to sell beer or other alcohol. He has married local girl Sarah Hukins who is now 24, but they don't seem to have any children. By virtue of the fact that 'The George' is not mentioned anywhere else, we assume that it is this property, especially as he has married the previous landlord's daughter!

**Elizabeth Hukins** (20) a farmer's daughter is visiting them. There were several families by the name of Hukins in Shalmsford Street at the time of the 1841 census, but none of them were called Elizabeth, so she could well be the wife of one of the sons. Also in the house is **Phoebe Norris** (69), an annuitant (pensioner) and **John Young** (31) who is listed as both a servant and an agricultural labourer. John was listed in 1841 as living in Shalmsford Street with his mother. Phoebe is a relative of Edward, I think, as one of his children is later called Norris.

The couple soon welcome their first son into the world, and I found in the parish records that Jesse Keeler was baptized on September 7th 1853. He is named Jesse after his grandfather, with the middle name Hukins.

'The George', which has been in existence from the 14th century building, was converted into flats in 2017, having been a public house for over 800 years.

## A Wheelwright

**Henry Wright** works as a carpenter and Jane (nee Gibson) looks after the home. Living with them are Mary Ann (16), Julia (14), George (12), Jane (3 months) and Henry (14). Henry may be an adopted son (he was born in Molash where the others were born in Chartham) or it may be they just forgot him when they were listing their family to the enumerator, so his name came last.

It is also interesting to note the discrepancy in ages from the oldest children to the youngest, which led me to check the date of their marriage. The records show that Henry and Jane were married in 1850, and that both Henry and Jane were widowed. Jane had been married to John Warden in 1835, but he passed away in 184. I cannot find details of Henry's first wife. Mary, Julia and George are Jane's children from her first marriage, and I wonder how they get on with their new step-father.

In 1852, baby Jane is joined by a brother, who is baptized in September as William Hobday Wright. Henry's specialism is given as wheelwright, an important job in a farming community including working on the mechanisms of the oast houses as well as on carts, waggons and carriages.

Their next chid, Charles is born in August 1855, but dies aged 9 months.

## Shalmsford Farmhouse

Shalmsford Farm, a farm of 180 acres, is now occupied by **Joseph Gambrill** (56), who was previously seen at Court Lodge Farm. He has five labourers in his employ. He was born near Elmsted and his wife, Sarah (58) comes from Brabourne. Their son John was born in Brabourne – perhaps Sarah went home to her mother for the birth of her first child? The other three children Thomas (20), Mary (18) and Jane (16) were born in Elmsted, presumably before the family moved to Shalmsford. John is learning the family business and will go on to take over the farm.

While Joseph works the land, Sarah is responsible for the servants and the dairy as well as day-to-day household management and care of her children.

The Gambrills have two farm servants, **William Hogben** (27) and **Thomas Young** (16) who live on-site. William is a local man, while Thomas came with the family from Elmsted. It is impossible to tell which of the local residents are the other farm workers.

In 1857 we read in the local newspaper, The Kentish Gazette, that the Chartham Agricultural Association held their annual ploughing match in a field near Shalmsford Farm on 2nd December and that the after-match dinner was provided by George Gambrill at 'The George'. Nineteen ploughing teams entered the match, which was judged by Mr Gambrill, Mr Epps and Mr Day. The time prize was won by S. Spillett, and I wonder if this is Stephen Spillett, recorded as living in Shalmsford Street at this time.

Other prizes were given out during the day, for such things as 'length of service' and 'bringing up a family without parochial relief', as well as for produce, e.g. hop samples.

## A Teacher

**Joseph Washford** (60) from Kingsnorth appeared in the 1841 census with his wife Sarah (now 58). He continues to work as an agricultural labourer, and his daughter Harriot (27) has found employment as a teacher. Also in the household is grandson **Joseph Andrews** (7). Young Joseph's mother is Frances. She marries Alfred Andrews, moves to Canterbury, and has nine children, while her parents stay in the village.

## Two Sawyers

The next resident in Shalmsford Street is **Stephen Cork** (52), a sawyer. His wife is no longer alive and he lives with his grown-up children. His son Henry (22) is an agricultural labourer and his daughter Ann (17) is expected to keep house. His nephew William. aged one, is living with them. Sawyers worked in pairs (one above and one below the saw pit) and Stephen probably worked with the other sawyer in Shalmsford Street, Charles Cook, although Stephen dies before the next census.

**Charles Cork** still works as a sawyer and is 67. He lives with his wife Elizabeth who is 65. Due to his age, I would think that he now operated in a supervisory capacity. Also on this census are Thomas Cook and Henry Cook, who are similar ages and would most likely work together. It looks like something of a family business!

## Brickmakers and Bricklayers

**John Adams** (57) is still married to Mary, who was born in Deal and is also fifty-seven. Their son Tritton (24) works as a bricklayer like his father and his wife Rebecca (nee Fearn) (24) (born at

Waltam) is at home. The young couple have only recently married and are yet to start their family. Through the census returns, we will see their family grow. I wonder whether this couple were married by way of the Kentish old custom recounted in The Invicta Magazine of 1908, where the first part of the marriage service is read in church when two people become engaged, so that only the remaining part is read during the actual marriage.

**George Burchett** (78) now lives on his own and also works as a journeyman bricklayer. He was not on the 1841 census and may have moved to Shalmsford Street to be near his sons. There is a burial record for a George Burchett of Shalmsford Street aged 81 in October 1856.

Jesse's brother **Philip Hukins** (57) shared a house in 1841, but now has his own household. He works as a journeyman bricklayer and lives with his wife Catherine (55). Two of Jesse's children, Philips's nieces Ann (10) and Lucy (8), are recorded as staying with them on the night of the census. Philip also owns or rents enough property to be on the Electoral Register

Jesse's other brother, **Thomas Hukins** (63) has expanded his business and is now a bricklayer employing eleven men. He still lives with his wife Mary Ann (47) from Cheriton and his children Thomas (19), Charles (15) and Harriot (10). Ambrose, (18) and James (14) are not mentioned, so they may be working elsewhere. Thomas is also on the Electoral Register.

The family is struck by tragedy when Harriet dies in 1854, aged 14, Thomas and Charles die in 1855 aged 23 and 19 respectively, and then Mary Ann follows them in 1856. Thomas remarries and by the time of the next census we see him still in Shalmsford, but living with his new wife, Marianne.

After some research, and noticing how important brick making is in the area, I have come to understand that the 'loam' referred to not gardeners loam, but in fact the type of clay known as brickearth, which was extracted all along the original path of The Stour, towards Pickleden. It was also taken from the hill above Box Trees House, which has resulted in a large depression next to The Slip.

After the top layer of loam has been removed, there is inevitably a layer of gravel or ballast underneath, which can also be harvested. The field previously mentioned is now known as 'The Old Ballast Pit'. The field immediately behind Irfon Bungalow was also known as a gravel pit, and the dip in the hill as it slopes down towards Court Lodge Farm is probably man-made. The site of the children's playground was also gravel pit, later filled in and transformed into a play area.

## Two Shoemakers

The next family is that of **George Burchett** (66), (AL), who lives with his extended family. In the house are his sister Mary (64) and his son Henry George (40) a cordwainer (shoemaker), with his wife Mary (43) and their son Henry (26) (AL). Henry Jr's wife is Eliza (26) who was born in Thanington as was their four-month-old son William. **Sarah Cork**, (64) who was born in Chilham, is visiting. 'George Burchett, Boot and Shoe Maker' appears in the 1858 Melville's Trade Directory, showing that he is regarded as a trusted professional.

The baptism records show a child called Ambrose baptized on February 6th 1855, the child of George and Mary Burchett, with the father's occupation is given as 'cordwainer'. The address of the parents is recorded as Loam Pits, Shalmsford Street.

**William Boulder** (48) is also a cordwainer (a shoe maker as opposed to a shoe mender) from Faversham and he is assisted in the business by his wife Sarah (46) whose occupation is listed as 'shoe binder'. Mary Ann Harris has now left.

Sarah's brother **John Rowland** (59) is now a widower and lives with them. He has found work as an agricultural labourer. The parish records show that a baby girl baptized Caroline is born to Mary Ann Rowland in 1855. I wonder if Mary Ann is John's daughter and has come to live with him for the birth.

After 20 years in the village, the couple move away before the next census.

## A Mix of Trades

The next family has three incomes. Firstly, from **Robert Harris** (60), who is a woodman and also from his daughter Sarah (25) who is a seamstress. The Harris's also enjoy an income from a lodger: **Thomas Fox** (79) is a retired shoemaker. A lodger is a person who rents a room but provides their own food. A boarder, by contrast, would eat with the family. The household is affluent enough to employ **Sarah Gurr** (44) as a housekeeper.

This group were together in 1841, and it is possible that Sarah means more to Robert than being just a housekeeper. Robert's daughter **Lavinia Worsley** (27) is visiting with her children Eliza Jane (2 years 11 months) and Robert Jonathan (10 months). Although Lavinia was born in Chartham, the children were not.

I found a burial record in the Chartham Parish Records for an Elsie or Eliza Harris, who is buried on 18th March 1857, who was living in Shalmsford Street. I think she might have been Robert's daughter.

## The Bakery and Grocer's Shops

**Phineas Shrubsole** (58) and his wife Ester (50) still run the bakery and grocers shop in the village. They still have no children, but their nephew **William Coppin Matthews** (5) lives with them and they still have one live-in servant, **Harriet Jarvis** (20) who was born nearby in Petham.

The bakery provided bread for the whole of Shalmsford, as only the farmhouses had ovens in their kitchens; the rest of the village cooked on open ranges until the introduction of the 'stove' towards the end of the century.

The field where this property sits is unmarked on the old tithe map, but is known locally as Longacre, and 41 Shalmsford Street is still known as 'The Old Bakery'.

The Old Bakery

Mr Shrubsole appears on the 1852 Electoral Register as Phineas Shrubsole Jnr., showing that his property is of sufficient size to allow him to vote. His brother Edward lives in Chartham, and his father, Phineas Shrubsole Snr lives in Canterbury. The business appears in the 1858 Melville's Trade Directory.

The couple never do have any children, but they remain central to the village of Shalmsford.

**John Homersham** (37) is a Grocer and Tea Dealer, and appears in the 1858 Melville's Trade Directory. His shop is in competition with that of Mr Shrubsole, a healthy rivalry that lasts for many years. He was born in Chartham, but his wife Elizabeth (37) was born in Little Mongeham, nr Deal. This couple did not appear on the 1841 census, but they were in the area, as their names appear on the church records at the baptism of their son George on 1st November 1848. With such an unusual name, I am sure he is related in some way to Thomas Homersham but I cannot fathom the relationship.

John and Elizabeth's son John Alfred is born in the summer of 1853, but dies aged 8 months.

## And on Bolts Hill we have:

### A House Painter

**William Goodale** (57) a painter who has moved to Bolts Hill from Wingham. He lives with his wife Mary (nee Hogben) (43) who was born in Godmersham. They have a large family and seem to have moved around the county, presumably in search of work for William. Their oldest sons James (20) and William (18) both work as plumbers. Together with the oldest daughter, Emma (16) who works as a dressmaker, these children were born in Margate. The others were born in Chartham and are: Ann (12), Frederick (10), George (8), Victoria (6), John (3) and Fanny (1). The family continue to live in the area and look after each other as they grow old.

James marries and has at least one child, James, born in 1854, before moving away from home.

The parish records of January 1855 show the baptism of Emma, daughter to Emma Goodale, a servant living on Bolts Hill. Later, the records of December 1857 show the baptism of baby Henry, born to Emma Goodale, spinster, of Bolts Hill.

There is also a record, in 1855, of the birth of a daughter to the unmarried Eliza Goodale. She calls him Alfred West Goodale, and I wonder if this is another grandchild for William. Unfortunately, he dies after 6 months.

The joy of these new members to the family is tempered by the deaths of George in April 1856 when he was 13 and William in 1857 aged 24.

### A Wheelwright

**William Cruttenden** (29) a journeyman wheelwright from Milton lives with his wife Sarah (30) a dressmaker from Lynsore (near Bishopsbourne). He will have worked hard to become qualified as the apprenticeship lasted up to five years. William's success continues and we see him later with a thriving business.

William needed to be an expert in wood types and quality as well as master craftsman. Wheels were made of seasoned elm, oak, ash or beech, with elm being chosen for hub, and oak for the spokes, cleft radially from a block, never sawn.

A wheelwright will have been responsible for making ploughs and harrows as well as wheels, waggons/ and carts.

## Another Sawyer

**Thomas Cook** (26) is a sawyer and lives with his wife Ann (30) **Sarah Pay** (77), a nurse, who is listed as a servant and would be living with them to help Ann after the birth of her son. The length of time she stayed would depend on need and the finances of the Cook household, but would generally be from ten days to four weeks, moving from living in to visiting daily before stopping her visits altogether.

## From Carrier to Landlord

**George Bourne** (35) lives on Bolts Hill with his wife Martha (35) who was born in Ramsgate and their daughter Elizabeth Ann (9). He works as a carrier. This family do well, as George takes over 'The George' pub from Stephen Goldup, while continuing to offer a carrier service. He stays in the property until the mid-1870s.

The beer sold at the pub was brewed on the premises and had a regulated alcohol content of up to 3%. Home brewed beer was half this strength and was watered down further for women and children.

## A Shoe Maker

Shoe making and mending was of tremendous importance, as shoes and boots were made to last at least a year, with heavy daily wear a necessity.

Next is the household of another shoemaker, **Thomas Woodland** (61) who was born in Ramsgate. His wife Frances, (48) was born in Chartham, so he moved here to be with her, or so that she was near her family. Their children are Elizabeth (18), Rachael (16) Isabella (14), William (11) and Samuel (9).

## A Second Schoolmistress

**James Govins** (26) lives with his wife Susan (26) in the next house. James comes from St Pancras in London as works as a paper glazier at the Paper Mill in in Chartham village. Susan is a school mistress at the Board School in Chartham.

## Two Gardeners

Next we see details for **James Stubberfield** (57) and his wife Ann (59). They now live with their daughter Marianne (34) and her son Jason (2 months) and James works as a gardener. James was born in Godmersham, but his wife and child were born in Chartham. Jason was born in Brabourn and as Marianne is listed as unmarried, the boy could her nephew. In the 1841 census, this family was living in the gardener's cottage at Court Lodge, and as his occupation has not changed, there is no reason to suppose that his address has, either.

**Joseph Stubberfield** (38) has taken over some of the gardening business from his father. Joseph has married his sweetheart Harriet (37) and they have three children, Joseph (8), Edwin (5) and Margaret (3). Over time, we see his business flourish.

# Agricultural Labourers

The families listed above are all ones in which the head of the household is employed in a specific trade or professions. The families listed below all fall into the category of agricultural labourers (AL). Again, I have followed the enumerator's lead and noted which live in Shalmsford Street and which live on Bolts Hill.

## Shalmsford Street

### Henry's Ready-Made Family

Another new household is the Amos family, and it is an interesting one. **Henry Amos** (29) (AL) is the head of the household. His wife Frances is 34. The first four children are George (12), Jane (10), Frances (8) and Emma (6) and they all have the surname Cozens and were born in Chilham. The youngest child Jesse, just 4 months old, has the surname Amos and was born in Chartham. Further investigation shows that Henry Amos married Frances Charlotte Cozens (formerly Horton) on 11th August 1850, so only Jesse is Henry's biological child, with the other children coming to the family from her previous marriage.

In the 1841 census, Henry was shown as sharing a house in Rattington Street, Chartham, with John Philpott's family and another boarder. Both boarders were male servants but John was an agricultural labourer. The census shows that John has just welcomed his first child into the world, so twenty-year-old Henry may have seen that as a good time to move on.

### A Growing Family

Next comes **William Philpott** (44) (AL) originally from Chilham, with his wife Harriette (35) and their children John (14), Mary (11), Sarah (9), George (7), Harriet (5), Jane (1). William previously lived in Box Tree Cottages in Bolts Hill but they have now moved into Shalmsford Street, perhaps because they were able to find a larger house to accommodate their growing family. The pair stay in the area as their family grows.

Harriette had to gets early in the morning to prepare breakfast for the family, as William needed to be at work at about 6am, with John and maybe with Mary and Sarah, although they could have started later after helping their mother in the house. Harriette prepared a packed lunch for William, probably bread, possibly with the addition of some jam or a small piece of cheese or cold meat, which he either taken with him or has brought to him by one of the younger children.

## Old Friends

**James Pay** (40) (AL) and his wife Frances (34) are also still in Shalmsford Street. Their daughter Frances is now 17 and no longer lives with them, but they have two more daughters Mary (9) and Jane (6). Thanks to the census we can track James and Frances' life through the years as they stay in the area and raise their family. Frances is six months pregnant at the time of the census, as their son James is baptized on June 9th 1851.

## A Home of his Own

**Stephen Spillett** (35), who we saw working as a servant at Court Lodge, now has his own household and works as an agricultural labourer. His wife Caroline (nee Dale) (28) looks after their children Esther (5) and Martha (19 months). The couple married in 1844 and go on to have two more children.

## Seven Children and Counting

Another familiar face is next. **George Hoare** (48) and his wife Mary (47) have kept their family with them, even though James and Harriet are old enough to be married. George and the oldest son James (23) work as agricultural labourers and the other children are at home: Harriet (17), Ellen (14), George (12), Sarah (10), Jesse (8), Emma (5), but I believe Jesse to be the son of George's brother Richard, not his own son. We continue to see this family over the coming years.

Son James does not appear on the next census, as he dies in 1853, aged 26.

## Help with the Grandchildren

George's father is the widower **Richard Hoare** (65) who still lives Shalmsford Street with his extended family. This is the same Richard Hoare recorded on the 1841 census as being sixty years old; the discrepancy is due to the rounding down of ages.

The household consists of Richard and his son Richard (46) who was born in Graveney; both men work as agricultural labourers. Richard Jnr's wife Eliza (nee Dodd) (39) was born in Chilham, as were all her children. The children are: Richard (15), James Mitchell (12), Phoebe (10) and Jesse (8). **Sarah Ann Clark** (15) and her sister Eliza (13) lodge with the Hoare family and work in the paper mill; both were born in Wickham.

## Workin' on the Railway

**Thomas Stickells** (32) and his wife Harriet (29) are new to the area. Thomas is a railway labourer, which is a new occupation. Their children are Thomas (9), Jane (7), Mary (6), Harriot (3) and Elizabeth (1). The family have two more children in Chartham; Stephen who is baptised in January 1852 and Richard, who is baptized on July 2nd 1854, and then they move to Folkestone, where Thomas easily finds work as a general labourer.

**William Brake** (or Banks) (31) from Brabourne also works as a railway labourer and lives with his wife Mary Ann (31) from Wye. Their first child Thomas (3) was born in Wye, but their seven-month-old boy William was born in Chartham. I have not found this family again.

## A Child Every Two Years

**William Newton** (40) (AL) still lives in Shalmsford Street. His wife Mary Ann (36) was born in Deal, and although their first daughter Mary Ann (14) was born in Chilham, the rest, Charlotte (10), Isaac (8), Sarah (6), Thomas (4) and John (1), were born in Chartham. They have two more daughters, Elizabeth in 1852 and Harriet in 1856. The two older children, William and John, have moved out.

This family is rather hard to follow, as there are several branches and the records are not complete. However, when William dies in 1856, the family move away.

## A Late Marriage

**Edward (37) (AL) and Eliza (39) Pay** also live in Shalmsford. They were married in 1845, when they were both working as servants. Edward gives his address as Shalmsford Street, and Eliza was living in Thruxted.

Edward and Eliza's son Edward is baptized on 2nd November 1851, but dies aged three, in 1854 and is buried on 20th November.

Their son George is christened on 6th November 1853, but also dies too young and is buried in 1855 aged 17 months.

## Two Women in the Kitchen

**Thomas Cork** (70) and his wife Sarah (nee Bass) (69) still live in Shalmsford Street. Their daughters have left home and their son **Henry** (27) has moved back in, bringing his new family with him. Thomas and Henry both give their occupation as agricultural labourers, and it is interesting to speculate on the role of Thomas in the workplace. Thomas was originally from Southstreet and Sarah was born in Chilham, but their children and grandchildren were born in Chartham. Henry's wife is 25-year-old Jane from Waltham. Their children are Henry (3) and Charlotte (1). Charlotte is not with the family long, as she dies in 1852.

Sarah dies in 1857 aged 75.

**William Baker** (51) (AL) lives with his wife Eliza (42) and their children Charlotte (13), Eliza (10), George (6) and Jane (2). The whole family were born in the village and continue to do so for some years. The family do lose one child, as George dies in 1856, aged 12 and he is buried in September.

## Supporting Their Unmarried Daughter

Another new-comer to the area is **Henry Banks** (52) (AL) is from Canterbury and his wife Sarah (50) from Lower Hardres. They share their home with their daughter Emilia (10). They must like it here, for they stay.

The parish baptismal records show that Amelia Banks gave birth to a daughter, Sarah Ann in May 1857, when she was 17, although she was not, at the time, married.

## Living Through the Death of a Baby

**William Friars** (37) (AL) from Harbledown is also new person to the village and lives with his wife Sarah (37). Sarah was born in Chilham as were their daughters Eliza (12) and Jane (6).

Again, this family stay in the village, even though they have to weather the death of a child. Frances is born in June 1855, but dies at 4 weeks and is buried in July. Perhaps the support they found in their neighbours at this difficult time encouraged them to stay.

## Their First Eight Children

**James Link** (46) (AL) was living in Shalmsford Street ten years earlier at the time of the 1841 census with his wife Jane (42) and five children ranging in age from twelve to six months. They now have seven living at home: Ann (21), John (15), Sarah (12), Maria (10), Edward (7), Henry (5) and George (3). James has left to set up a home of his own and John, at 15 is now working as an apprentice. Ann marries William Fisher in 1855, and may already be courting at the time of this census. With so many children, it is not surprising that many of them make their home here, near their parents.

Jane is already pregnant with another child, and her daughter Jane is baptized in December 1851. She is joined in motherhood by her daughter Ann, who gives birth to Hester in January 1852, but Ann's baby dies aged two.

## Planning for Old Age

**Richard Mongeham** (61) (AL) lives with his wife Mary (62) but by 1861, his wife has died and he lives with his daughter Sarah. His son Thomas lives in the street, but not necessarily next door, and Mary loves it when her grandson James comes to visit.

## A New Family

**James Austin** (27) (AL) has moved to the village from Denton. His wife Sarah (28) and his daughter Angelina (6 months) were both born in Chilham. Sarah will not be working alongside her husband now she has a young child to look after, but will be taking in some kind of piece work to earn extra money. She will be up before dawn to prepare his breakfast and pack his mid-day meal, and have a smaller evening meal ready when he comes home after dusk. Few houses had ovens, and cooking was done on an open fire or on a range, so the meal was a stew of some kind with hunks of bread and lots of potatoes.

## Income From a Lodger

**Thomas Mongeham** (37) and his wife Ann (35) supplement his wages as an agricultural labourer by taking in a lodger, **Edward Holmes** (21) a journeyman baker from Harbledown. Their eleven-year-old son James also still lives with them and Richard and Mary who live in the street are Thomas' parents. In 1859 10s is awarded to Ann Mongeham by the committee of the Chartham Agricultural Association as she is a widow.

## At the end of a Happy Life

**John Hulse** is now 72 and has still recorded his occupation as agricultural labourer. He lives with his wife Ann (68). Ten years earlier, they had shared their dwelling with the Hukins family, but they now live on their own. I cannot find where John goes after the 1851 census; Ann dies in October 1859 aged 77.

## Living Next Door to Mum

Next is **Mary Warden** (75) who describes herself as a labourer's widow and is a pauper but she is the head of her household. A person who defined themselves as a pauper could possibly be destitute, but was not necessarily. Being in receipt of poor relief meant that they were able to claim other benefits.

Next door is a **Charles Warden** (31), and his wife Emma (34) who were recorded in 1841 with no children. Charles still works as an agricultural labourer and Emma has her hands full with children George (9), William (7) James (5) and Eliza (3). Charles could be Mary's son.

## Dealing with the Death of His Wife

**William Loram** (56) (AL) lives in the next house recorded and is now a widower, as his wife died just a year after the last census. He has four children living with him. Mary (21) keeps house and looks after her siblings William (15), Eliza (12) and Elizabeth (10). The boys George (19) and Jesse and Charles (18) have now left home. The youngest child, Michael is no longer listed as he died in 1844, and was buried in Chartham on June 8th of that year. Elizabeth is William's granddaughter.

The parish records show the baptism of Sarah, born to Mary Loram, spinster, in 1852. Mary already has one illegitimate child and this seems to be another. Sadly the baby dies in 1854 and is buried on 23rd March. An illegitimate child born in the Victorian era almost always had a poor outlook, mainly due to pressures on the Mother to work, making her unable to breastfeed. The child was then often fed cow's milk or pap (bread and water), which was of poor nutritional value.

I have also found the baptism of a child called Elizabeth and it shows Eliza Loram as her mother. The date is 1856, and it shows the address of the mother as Box Trees, presumably Box Tree Cottages. This would make William's daughter, Eliza, the seventeen-year-old mother.

The register of 1859 show that Elizabeth Arbin Loram then gave birth to Edward Beaney, who was baptized on August 7th. This seems to be the beginning of a new family, as we can also see that Edmund Beaney and Elizabeth Arbin Loram married in 1863. Edmund was 20 years older than Elizabeth, and was listed as a bachelor on the parish records. His occupation was given as 'labourer'.

## A Lively Family

**James Austen** (40) from Westbere is married to Elizabeth (nee Hoare) (38) from Chartham, and they live with their large family in Shalmsford Street. Elizabeth is niece to Richard Hoare, formerly mentioned, who is her father's brother.

**Thomas Hoare** (75), Elizabeth's father, lives with them and both men are agricultural labourers, supporting Elizabeth and seven children. Mary (13), Ann (11), Ellen (9), James (7), Elizabeth (5), Charlotte (3) and baby Edward (16 months) all live in the one house. Already firmly established in the area by his marriage to one of the Hoare girls, James and his family stay here for many years.

Thomas dies within the year, and is buried on 18th April 1852.

## A New Wife for Frederick

**Frederick Spillett** (23) (AL), brother to Stephen, and his wife Ann (nee Tanner) (24) were married in 1849 but do not yet have any children, although Ann is already pregnant and their daughter Eliza Ann is baptized on November 17th 1851. On the next census we find that they have moved to Harbledown and have four children.

## Happy Together

**William Hayward** (65) (AL) and his wife Thomazin (57) share a house together but the boys they were fostering have moved on. The couple continue to live together for at least another ten years.

## Grandad's in Charge

**John Marsh** (72) was born in Wattisham and lives with his grand-daughter **Sarah Spickett** (8). This information leads us to conclude that he is father to John Marsh and Sarah Spickett, whom we saw in 1841. He lists his occupation as labourer. John dies a few years later, aged 76 and is buried in St Mary's on 14th May 1857. Sarah at 15 would need a guardian in today's world, but in 1851 she was able to work full time to support herself.

## A Long and Happy Life

**Ann Young** (75) is a widow and lives on her own. Her sons William and John have left home. She was born in Crundale, and dies in 1959 aged 80.

# Bolts Hill

It is significant to note that there are many more households living on Bolts Hill than there were ten years previously as the area as the top of the hill is turned over to residential housing. Even within living memory, the area supported hop fields and arable crops. Today, it is almost totally covered with housing.

## A Lucrative Trade

The next dwelling recorded is Box Trees, home to **Thomas Gibson** (65) and his wife Mary (nee Cook) (65). Thomas works as a labourer for a carrier, presumably George Bourne. Although not strictly an agricultural labourer, he falls more correctly within this category than in the 'trades and professions' section. When Mary dies in 1857, the burial record shows her address as Box Tree House, a sixteenth-century building that is now Grade II listed.

## A Thirteen-Year-Old Housewife

**John Barker** (45) is an agricultural labourer. This may or may not be the same John Barker recorded in the 1841 census in Shalmsford Street. If it is, his wife Mary has died and the four elder children have moved away. Ann (13) is now in charge of the house along with Elizabeth (11). Two more children, Eliza (9) and Ann (5) have been added to the family.

Anne's life was a tough one, but at least she would not have been sent away into service. She go up before dawn to boil water for tea and to prepare dinner for those members of the family working in the fields, including herself. Breakfast was usually a bowl of bread, seasoned with salt and wetted with hot water – a poor man's version of bread-and-milk, when milk was too expensive for the average family to afford. There might also have been a cup of tea if someone was up early enough to light a fire in order to boil the water; alternatively, a glass of beer was the only real option.

When Anne joined the family working in the fields during the day, she left work an hour or two early to walk home and prepare the evening meal, wrapping her shawl tightly around her as the weather dictated.

## Three Generations

**Elizabeth Vincer** (now 60) was recorded on the 1841 census as the head of the household, but she dies before the next census, in 1859. She still lives with her daughter Elizabeth (41) and Elizabeth's son Charles (21). Mary is no longer in the house. Charles is an agricultural labourer while Elizabeth Snr records herself as a pauper. This family is an interesting one, and stays in the locality.

## A Single Mother

**Frances Spillett** (nee Vincer) (37) lives with her son George (7). She appeared on the 1841 census living with her husband Joseph and daughter Eliza (then 1), with her mother, but she is now a widow and is head of her own household. The mathematicians amongst you may have worked out that George was born too long after his father's death to be a Spillett, but the truth about his parentage will never be known. Eliza and Spillett are both common names in the area, so it is hard to follow the life of Eliza, but there is a death record for Eliza Spillett in 1848, which could be this child.

## Another Full House

**James Friar** (26) (AL) has a full house. He lives with his wife Eliza (26) and his son James (6) but also has Eliza's father **John Philpott** (72) living with them as well as a lodger. John lists his occupation as agricultural labourer and the lodger, **George Cork** (41) is a pensioner.

## Two Williams

Further along are two Williams. **William Cousins** (69) and his son **William Cousins** (32) both work as agricultural labourers while William Snr's wife Sarah (68) looks after the house. The family are still here on the 1861 return.

## A Family Man

**Thomas Newington** (49) (AL) was born in Harbledown and has recently moved his family from Shalmsford Street to Bolts Hill. His wife Ann (nee Court) (43) was born in nearby Blean. Their daughter Amelia (26) is a dressmaker and is their oldest child, having been born a year after their marriage. A cousin is also staying with them; **Sarah Hills** (77) is the widow of an agricultural labourer; she was born in Patrixbourne.

Thomas has done well for himself, and is recorded on the 1852 Electoral Register, showing that he owns a considerable amount of property, although not yet 'The Cross Keys' Pub, which he takes over in 1859. This property has since been divided into two residential houses, Cross Keys Lodge and Cross Keys Cottage.

## Aunt Sarah Comes to Stay

From a tiny household, we move to a much larger one. **William Philpott** (40) lives with his wife Ann (35), his sister **Sarah Smith** (33) and a lodger **Henry Spillett** (23) with his wife Sophia (Hoare) (20), who goes on to become one of the village's schoolmistresses. Her parents are George and Mary Hoare, mentioned on the last census return. The two men work as agricultural labourers. The Philpotts have five children: Sarah (13), Lidia (11), Mary (9), George (6) and Eliza (4), and have another is soon on the way. Sarah Ann is baptized in February 1852. The couple also have sons, Charles, in 1854 and James in 1855. Their address is given as Box Trees.

William dies in 1857 and is buried on 24th September 1857. Ann is listed as Anny on the 1861 census.

## Just the Two of Us

Close by, but listed as a separate household is **Richard Gibson** (59) (AL) and his wife Elizabeth (nee Cudham) (56).

## Box Tree Cottages

Next are **William Gibson** (23) (AL) and his wife Sarah (nee Hill) (23). Their baby son G. H. Albert is just five months old. The family soon move to Bolts Hill and stay in the Shalmsford area. Their next child, Frances Phillis is baptized on February 6th 1853 and son Jesse in 1854. In each case the address is given as Box Trees.

Another agricultural labourer is in the next house, too. **John Marsh** (32) from Chartham has married Ann Austen (22) from Westbere and they live with their daughters Charlotte (8) and Ann (4). As with other wives in this census, Ann must have been married at 16. We will later see the girls grow up and marry. Charlotte is already dressed in almost identical clothes to her mother, with long skirts and a corset worn daily.

**George Cork** (35) (AL) is married to Eliza (38) from Waltham. Their daughter Charlotte (13) was born in Crundale, but subsequent children Sarah (10), Ann (8), Henry (3) and William (1 month) were born in Chartham. The 1841 census showed his wife's name as Mary, but with only one child, Charlotte, recorded, it is hard to decide if that is the same family or a different one.

There is a baptism record for Fanny Cork in 1850, to parents George and Elizabeth. Unfortunately, this good news is short-lived as she dies the same year.

When William was born, the church records show the family living in Bolts Hill. George and Eliza have a hard year ahead of them as Charlotte, who has survived the dangerous years of early childhood, dies aged 14 later this year. She is buried on July 30th. The couple are further struck by tragedy in 1853, when their son Edward dies at the age of 5 weeks and again in 1857, when Ann dies aged 14.

## Other Records

As before, many people come and go into and out of the area over the decade, and not all are here at the time of the census. Some of the people who are missing are:

- Baby Edward Cork, of Bolts Hill, who is buried in March 1853 aged 5 weeks; I cannot find the names of his parents.

- William Cook also from Bolts Hill who died in November aged 9 weeks.

- John Cork who was living in Shalmsford Street at the time of his death in 1854 aged 34.

- Another death in the Cork family was that of Thomas Cork, who lived on Bolts Hill and died in 1859 at 6 months old. His parents were Thomas and Ann Cork.

- And finally for this family, Fanny Cork also died in 1859, aged 2. I could not find how or if these children are related.

- Another child who died too young was Walter Frederick Cork who was buried on 26h February 1854.

- Joseph and Louisa Collard's son John was christened in St Mary's in July 1855, but the couple returned to the church in October, when he was buried aged 3 months. This family do not appear on the census records for the village.

- Thomas Brooks was buried on 10th March 1956, aged 8. Again, his address was recorded as Shalmsford Street.

- Sarah Park's burial record on 26th October 1856 also shows her address as Shalmsford Street. She was 16, but I do not know if she lived on her own, was a servant, or whether she lived with her parents.

- Mary Ann Vidgen of Bolts Hill who was buried on 23rd July 1857 aged 2 years 1 month. The 1847 edition of Bagshaw's Directory of Kent Vol II, gives the name of Hammond Vidgen as a tailor. Perhaps Mary Ann was his child?

- John Mutton lived in Shalmsford Street at the time of his death in 1859, aged 66.

However, there is some good news, as there is evidence that a further eight babies were born in the area between the census returns.

- There is a baptism record for a boy called Robert Thomas who was born to Jane Blanche dated 5th October 1851. The girl does not appear on the census, but is listed on the baptism return as a servant. She is unmarried. Unlike many illegitimate children of this time, he thrives. At the time of the 1851 census, Jane was recorded as being 22 and working in Canterbury as a housemaid.

- Mary Jane Albina Castle is born in the summer of 1852 to John and Charlotte Frances Castle, but she dies aged just 2.

- William and Mary Ann Brooks welcome Elizabeth into their family in July 1852. I wonder if these are the parents of Thomas, listed above as a death in 1856? They also have a son, Charles, in September 1854 and a daughter Charlotte in 1856.

- James Henry and Julia Hearn have a baby called Julia Susanne in 1856, but they do not stay in the area. James works as a bailiff.

- Julia Warden, a spinster from Shalmsford Street, has her baby George christened on 2nd May 1858. Julia appeared on the 1841 census aged 4, living with her mother Jane. Julia is 21 at the time of George's birth, stays in the area.

- Clarissa, daughter of George and Clarissa Fearn from Bolts Hill is baptized in July 1859

- Elizabeth Ann is baptized in August 1859, and is the daughter of Mary Ann Bowles.

- Another member of the Link family is living in the area around this time, as I found a baptism for Edward, son of John and Caroline Link of Box Trees in January 1860. The baby will have been born in 1859, and he is the grandson of James and Jane Link

- The Melville's Trade Directory listing shows us the tradespeople living in Shalmsford Street at the time. Some are those we find on the 1851 census, but some have moved into the area in the intervening seven years. Those who appear in the trade directory, but are not on the census are:

- William Foreman, Carpenter and Wheelwright, who we will later meet again.

- Stephen Goldup, who takes over 'The George'

- Joseph Shaddleton, a farmer

Shalmsford Street, looking northwards from the railway bridge, with Fern Cottages on the right. The waste ground to the left has still not been developed.

# 1860s

There were many improvements in the life of the rural community in the mid-1800s, including the introduction of paraffin for use as lighting in place of candles, and the repeal of the window tax 1851. Most importantly for a rural area like Shalmsford, a law was passed in 1867 to prevent children working in agricultural gangs. They were still involved in agricultural work on a regular basis, but were spared the pressure of being under the control of a demanding gang master.

The railway company has now erected a station at Chartham, making travel a real possibility for working class people. The Kentish Chronicle of 1865 published the train times, and it is not without some cynicism that I note the fact that the 8.08am train from Chartham arrives at Charring Cross at 10.35am, a time of just under two and a half hours. This must have seemed incredible to the people of the day, and they would not have known that, despite the improvements in the rail system, this is still not very far from the travel time in the 21st Century.

Parish Road was completed this decade, which saved residents the trouble of crossing and re-crossing the railway line. The bridge across The Stour was erected in 1862, and there is a plaque on the upstream side which confirms this.

The 1860s started off badly in terms of weather, with snow throughout almost the whole of January in 1864, 1866 and 1867. This was matched by the heat in the summer of 1868, which was the longest, hottest summer on record until 1976. Temperatures in Tonbridge reached over 38 degrees.

One of the most divisive topics of conversation during this decade was the start of the American Civil War, which split opinion throughout the county. Another, closer to home, was the introduction of the new hymn book, Hymns Ancient and Modern, now being used by the Church of England.

## The 1861 Census

The 1861 census for Shalmsford Street was taken by George Baker Ruff and detailed those in each household on the night of 7th April. Enumeration District 2 for the Chartham area comprised: that part of Chartham parish 'situated on the south side of the River Stour including Perry Court Farm, Thruxted Farm, Underdown Cottages, Mystole House and Cottages, Longneck Cottage, Pickleden Farm and Cottage, Shalmsford Street Gate House and Cottage, Shalmsford Street, Bolts Hill, Box Trees Road, The Deanery, Court Lodge, The Grange, Rattington Street, Horton Chapel Farm and Cottages and Chartham Downs Farm Cottages.'

George was a farmer living in Rattington Street at the time, and with a large farm to manage, one wonders how much of the enumeration he undertook himself. I suspect he asked one of his employees to give out and collect the returns, after which he entered the information into the enumeration book. We can see that George was just the type of careful person who enjoyed filling in the information, as on his own return he gives his occupation as 'Farmer of 119 acres employing 4 men, 2 boys, 4 women regular' but qualifies this information by explaining that this is 'independent of occasional extra help'. This seems a bit pedantic, but thank goodness for people who did enter such detailed descriptions!

The age range of people living in the village has stayed stable over the last ten years, with approximately the same number of under-10s (74) and the same number of 70-80 year olds (12), although the number of separate households has increased slightly, to 75.

The wages for an agricultural labourer have actually decreased over the past twenty years, and have now reached an all-time low, before increasing again in the 1870s. The average national wage for this occupation is 13s per week, but that in Kent is significantly lower – higher wages in the north of the country have skewed the figures. The following is a suggested budget for a family earning 13 shillings per week (s = shillings, d = pence) taken from the book *'My Ancestor was an Agricultural Labourer'*:

| Rent | 1s 6d |
| School | 4d |
| 6 Candles | 5d |
| Soap | 2s ½ d |
| Coal/fuel | 1s |
| Bread (4lb per person per day) | 4s 8d |
| Cheese | 4d |
| 3lb Meat | 2s |
| Tea/1.5lb sugar | 1s 3d |
| Treacle used instead of butter (8d/lb) | 3d |
| Benefit society | 1s |
| Tobacco | 4d |

If you were a Kentish housewife and had 3s less, where would you make the cuts? Quite often, the very poorest people let their benefit society subscription lapse, which is equivalent to living without life insurance or health insurance – a risky path indeed in the days before The National Health Service. On top of this, a labourer needed to provide his own tools and to have clothing that was fit for purpose. A pair of boots cost 15s. As you can see, life without the income of a wife and children was hardly possible.

There are now even more households in the Shalmsford Street/Bolts Hill area, and we can see that the type of work undertaken is gradually changing. More people are engaged in specific jobs than ever before.

I view these job descriptions with several reservations. One is that the person giving the information may have wanted to over-state the importance of their position to impress either the enumerator or other people in the room at the time

It is also possible to gain a false impression of village life if we take the types of employment at face value. At the beginning of the Victorian era, men worked where they lived, travelling only if they were agricultural workers, whose place of work was at the ends of an estate. However, by 1860, a blacksmith might live in one village but work in another, taking the train into the nearest town or even another village each day. Thus, the number of certain tradesmen does not necessarily mean that the trade was carried out in the village. Mr Pollard the watchmaker, for instance, may well have worked in Canterbury, not Shalmsford.

## Trades and Professions

To reflect the information given on the census returns, I have presented the information in two sections: Shalmsford Street and Bolts Hill.

## Shalmsford Street

### Two Carpenters

First are **James Pay** (50) and his wife Ann (49), who was born in Selling, their son Benjamin (13) and their daughter Sarah (10). James is a journeyman carpenter. Both Benjamin and Sarah go to school, which is a reflection of James' status and income that he can afford to keep a boy in school this long.

Occupations in Shalmsford, 1861

| Occupation | Count | % |
|---|---|---|
| Agricultural Labourer | 66 | 47% |
| Carpenter/joiner | 7 | 5% |
| Domestic servant | 7 | 5% |
| Shoe maker | 6 | 4% |
| Carter/mate | 5 | 3% |
| Bricklayer | 4 | 3% |
| Bricklayer's labourer | 4 | 3% |
| Dressmaker/seamstress | 4 | 3% |
| House painter | 3 | 2% |
| Sawyer | 3 | 2% |
| Wood dealer | 3 | 2% |
| Apprentice to trade | 2 | 1% |
| Builder | 2 | 1% |
| Grocer | 2 | 1% |
| Publican/victualler | 2 | 1% |
| Baker | 1 | <1% |
| Baker | 1 | <1% |
| Coal merchant | 1 | <1% |
| Dealer in cattle | 1 | <1% |
| Drover | 1 | <1% |
| Engine Driver | 1 | <1% |
| Farmer | 1 | <1% |
| Milliner | 1 | <1% |
| Nurseryman/florist | 1 | <1% |
| Nurseryman/seedsman | 1 | <1% |
| Ostler | 1 | <1% |
| Paper maker | 1 | <1% |
| Railway servant | 1 | <1% |
| Teacher | 1 | <1% |
| Watchmaker | 1 | <1% |
| Wheelwright | 1 | <1% |
| | 139 | |

The Pay's daughter Susannah is not mentioned on this census, even though she was listed in 1851, when she was five years old. The parish records show the birth of James Horton Pay to Susannah

Pay in the summer of 1867, and I can be fairly certain that this is the same girl, as Susannah is not a common name in this area. Her address is recorded as Shalmsford Street, so we can assume she had already moved out by the time of this census in 1861. The story has a happy ending when we see that Susannah married James Horton and can be found on the 1871 census living in Chilham with her husband, son and new baby, Isabella.

The next household is relatively affluent. **Charles Ruck** (46) still works as a carpenter. He lives with his wife Matilda (45) and their children William (21), Frederick (18) and Lavinia (10). The family stay in the village and we will be able to follow their progress through the decades, including the birth of their grandchildren.

Frederick was not on the 1851 census, as he was staying with his Aunt Agnes, for whom his sister was named. His sister Agnes, who we saw on the 1851 census, is now working as a servant in Rattington Street, Chartham, and Hannah is now going by the name Lavinia.

William gives his marital status as 'married', but no wife is mentioned. He works as a carpenter and Fredrick works as an agricultural labourer; Lavinia goes to school.

Further investigation shows that William has married Maria Smith, and that she is staying at Mystole Green with her parents on the night of the census with her son William Ruck (1). The family are living together in Shalmsford Street at the time of the next census.

A parish record of 1863 gives the baptism details of Walter Charles, son of William and Maria Ruck. He lives for three years, before his death in 1866.

Charles' sister-in-law **Amelia Long** (44) from Bishopsbourne is staying, but is listed as a boarder, so I assume she is either a spinster previously looking after aged parents, or a widow.

## Shalmsford Farm House

**Joseph Gambrill** (65) is a farmer of 165 acres employing four labourers and one boy. His wife Sarah (66) helps on the farm. His children John (31), Mary (27) Jane (24) and Catherine (30) who is his daughter-in-law (wife of John) have entered son or daughter of famer as their occupation, indicating that they are part of the monied class who do not work. Thomas has left home.

Catherine in already pregnant with her next child, and Eliza Ann is baptized in November 1861. This joy is balanced by the fact that Sarah dies in 1866 at her home in Shalmsford Street. Her husband Joseph moves in with his daughter Mary after Catherine's death and dies in 1879.

The family have two servants, **William Arnold** (20) who was born in Godmersham and is a carter and **James Warden** (18) who is a carter's mate. They are recognisable by their whips and smock coats. I suspect that James, as the youngest, was the one who had to make sure the wagon box, resting on the rail at the side of the wagon was well-stocked with a packed lunch (the main meal of the day) and a good supply of cold tea.

## The Publican

At 'The George' is **George Bourne** (45) who is both publican and postmaster. He lives with his wife Martha (45), who helps run the pub, and his daughter Elizabeth (19), a milliner. **Charles Arnold** (16) lives in the pub and works as an ostler and male servant. George was previously recorded living on Bolts Hill working as a carrier, a business that he continues while at 'The George'.

As the census is taken in the spring of 1861, George may already be planning the annual dinner of the Chartham Benefit Club. The previous dinner, in 1860, was reported in the Kentish Chronicle on 9th June 1860:

CHARTHAM. ANNUAL DINNER.

*The members of the Chartham Benefit Club, held at Mr. George Bourne's, the "George Inn," dined together on Saturday. Upwards of 140 sat down to an excellent repast, served up in capital style. Mr. George Hayward (president) occupied the chair. The state of the weather prevented the company from joining in out-door games; but this circumstance only added to the spirit and conviviality that prevailed in the club-room. The usual division of the surplus took place. Every one present appeared well pleased with the result of their Annual gathering.*

Many villages had benefit clubs of this kind, which were funded by subscription which were intended to give relief to the poor in times of need. Prior to the dinner, members gathered outside the pub and processed around the village, carrying their club banner, almost certainly accompanied by music to drum up support from both potential members and potential donors.

George Bourne and his family left 'The George' soon after the census was taken to manage The Bear and Key in Whitstable. He took out an advertisement in The South Eastern Gazette in July 1863 in which he thanked his 'numerous friends and customers who supported him in his late business at 'The George' Inn, Shalmsford Street'.

The inn and associated fly and carrier business was taken over by Oliver Gould in 1863, who had previously been a tailor. He, too, took out an advertisement in the local paper, notifying friends and the public that he was now incumbent, and hoped that by attention to his business and by supplying first-class refreshments at moderate prices he might secure their support. He intended to carry on his tailoring business as well as those of publican, carter and fly proprietor.

## Shoemakers and Menders

**Thomas Beaney** (30), cordwainer, is head of a large household. He lives with his wife Emma (nee Philpott) (29) who works with him in the shoe making business. Their children are Mary (9), William (7), Matilda (5), Jane (3), Thomas (2) and John (3 months). Only Mary and William attend school. **William Scott** (15) boards with the family while working as an apprentice.

A cordwainer was responsible for making and mending harnesses as well as making shoes.

Thomas seems to have found life hard and resorted to drink on more than one occasion. In the newspaper of May 1865 it is reported that the judge at the St Augustine's Petty Sessions found him guilty of being drunk and abusive to Police Sergeant Chard at Shalmsford Street on 27th May. He was fined 5 shillings and 11 shillings costs.

**George Philpott** (28) and Amelia (nee Banks) (21) have one young son, Henry, aged just two months, who was christened John Henry, but is known as just Henry. George is a shoemaker and the couple married in 1858. Amelia dies later this year, and is buried on November 17th. George remarries in 1866, choosing Emily Reynolds. The couple move to Barham and by 1871 have five children of their own.

The next residence is that of **George Gilham** (26) and his wife Sarah (28). George is a shoe maker from High Halden, and Sarah works as a dressmaker. **Mary Mongeham** (74) is James' mother-in-law and contributes to the household with her wages from working as an agricultural labourer. She was living with her husband Richard in Shalmsford Street, at the time of the 1851 census. This family do not stay in the area.

As well as producing shirts and dresses, Sarah would have been asked to provide undergarments to support these. The plain-sewing of a chemise or nightgown was not beyond the skill of the housewife, but creating a stable corset (worn by women of all classes throughout the Victorian era) was now becoming more of a craft. Corsets were even provided as part of the uniform of asylums and workhouses, much as a bra is today.

## Two Builders

**Thomas Hukins**, (73) is still a builder, now employing 13 men - two more than in 1851. He lives with his wife Marianne (45), who he married in 1858 after the death of his first wife, Mary, in 1856. Also in the house is his eleven-year-old stepson James Stubberfield, who is still in school. Thomas and Marianne were born in Chartham, but James was born in Canterbury. Thomas dies in 1864, leaving £200 in his will.

One particular Act of Parliament that will have pleased Thomas and increased his profits was the repeal of the Window Tax in 1851. This had been imposed in 1695 and demanded a tax similar to stamp duty on each window in a house. After 1851, an unrestricted number of windows could be added to a home, making it more attractive to look at and to live in. Such a house would command a higher price, which was good news for a builder such as Thomas Hukins. The general population were not freed from tax, however, as a tax on inhabited buildings replaced the Window Tax.

The next household is that of **Alfred Foreman** (35) from Hernehill. We are now seeing more people coming in from outside and also marrying outside their parish. Alfred's wife Jane (30) was born in Sheldwich. Alfred is a builder employing one man and one boy. Their only son Frank (6) was born in St Dunstans, Canterbury and is listed as a scholar. We are beginning to see a pattern here of school attendance, which applies to the wealthier families only. Until the Education Act of 1870, it was not compulsory for children to attend school and it was often the few pennies they earnt that made the difference to the families living comfortably or not.

There is one visitor staying with them on the night of the census, a **Sarah Bartlett** (37) from Sheldwich, Jane's home town. Their house is large enough to accommodate three boarders, **Thomas Munse** (22) from Aldington, **Henry Stokes** (23) from Nonnington and **George Ralph** (17) from Staple. All three young men work as carpenters and joiners, with George noting that he is an apprentice.

Alfred stays in Shalmsford and becomes something of a mover-and-shaker within the local community. There are constant references to him in the local newspapers in the reports of the planning committee and he sits on more than one local committee himself. He also turns out to be something of a local worthy, leading community initiatives and promoting innovative ideas on labour management.

In 1867, we read in The Kentish Chronical that a builder's shop has been used as the venue for the Choral Society's fourth annual recital. The builder's shop was 'handsomely decorated' for the evening, which lasted from 7.45pm until 10.30pm, including both secular and sacred music. This is one of the first of the many reports we read about Alfred.

## Three Bricklayers

**Philip Hukins** (62) still works as a bricklayer, presumably for his builder brother Thomas, and lives with his wife Catherine (65). Catherine dies in 1867, and Philip continues to live here until his death in 1876.

**John Adams** (62) is a bricklayer. His wife Mary (62) was born in Deal. His son Tritton and his wife have moved out now.

Thomas keeps working and the family stay here for many years.

**James Tritton Adams** (36) is a bricklayer and has now moved out of his parents' home. James' wife Rebecca (35) was born in the nearby hamlet of Waltham and they have two children: Robert Tritton (3) and Harriett (1). It seems odd that James Tritton is recorded using the name James on this census, whereas on all the others the enumerator has put Tritton. James may have hated the name Tritton and insisted on being called James or vice versa. James has been a bricklayer since we first met him at the age of 15, working with his father.

## A Watchmaker from Whitstable

**Samuel D. Pollard** (24), a watchmaker, was born in Whitstable and after his apprenticeship in Deptford is now fully qualified. His wife Hannah (30) was born in Radnorshire in Wales. Their one-year-old daughter Ellen was born in Dunninston in Kent. They only stay here a short while, and by 1871 have moved on again, this time to Upper Hardres. The movement of this family disproves the widely-held belief that Victorian families rarely left their home town.

## A Sawyer

**Henry Cook** (32) was born in Chartham and is a sawyer. His wife, Charlotte (28), is from nearby Petham. They have one daughter, Lydia (5), who goes to school. The next child, Caroline is born in 1863, and dies 8 months later.

## Two Gardeners

**James Stubberfield** (77) from Thanington is, as we know, a nurseryman and seedsman and he has now taken on the role of local preacher, either at the Wesleyan Methodist Church on Bolts Hill or the Primitive Methodist Church in Shalmsford Street. His wife Ann (79) is from Godmersham.

Both James and Ann enjoy being close to their son Joseph Stubberfield (47) who is also a nurseryman and florist. He lives with his son Edwin (15) and his daughter Mary (13). Both children attend school, which is an indication of how successful the family business has become. Joseph's wife is not listed here, but she does appear on subsequent surveys, and his oldest son has moved out of the family home.

## Two Dealers in Wood

**William Vidgeon** (42), a wood dealer from Wye lives in the next residence with his wife Sarah (37), who assists him in the business. Sarah was born in Crundale and their eldest daughter Harriet (13) was born in Thanington. The second two children Emma (10) and Georgina (8) were born in Chartham; all three girls attend school. William and Sarah's son George is just 9 months old. Harriet goes on to marry Edward Hoare in 1869.

There is a gap in the ages of the children, as the couple have lost at least one child. Mary Ann was born in 1855 and died in 1857. The couple are recorded as living on Bolts Hill at the time, and are still there in 1863 when their son Reuben is born.

**Edward Vidgeon** (38), also a wood dealer from Wye lives with his wife Charlotte (33) from Selling. Charlotte helps Edward in the business. Edward and Charlotte have five children: Anne (10) and James (9) were born in Canterbury, while Clara (6), Albert (3) and Thomas (1) were born in Chartham. Caroline is born in 1862, but dies in 1867, so does not appear on any census. The couple also have a son, Austin in 1869 before they move away.

James goes on to marry Emily Hoare but Anne dies in 1866. She is buried on December 27th, aged just 17.

## In the Building Trade

**John Keeler** (26) is a bricklayer's labourer from Waltham, a few miles away. His wife Sarah (24) is from Lyminge and works as an agricultural labourer. Their children are George (5) and Mary (9 months). George is shown as being a scholar. The family soon move away to Sturry, where they have three more children, but not until after the birth of their son John in 1863.

## The Grocers Shop

Next is the more affluent household of **John Homersham** (48) and his wife Elizabeth (47). They still run a grocers and coal merchant business. Their children are George (14) and Mary (12), who both attend school. **Emma Cozens** (18) lives with them and works as a general servant. Their business continues to flourish for many years.

## The Village Stores

**Phineas Shrubsole** (68) is now a baker and grocer's master employing one man. His wife Esther, from the Isle of Wight, is now 62 and their nephew, **William Matthews** (15) still lives with them. **Sophie Harris** (20) from Broughton lives with them and works as a general servant. Ten years later, he is still working in Shalmsford.

**William Cozens** (48) lives with his wife Ann (44) and Ann's son William Kemp who is 14 and still at school. Ann was born in Shrivenham in Berkshire, so I wonder what brought her to Kent. William works as a gardener.

## A Railway Employee

Railway Gate House is home to **Obediah Soloman** from Ewhurst in Sussex (32) who describes himself as a 'railway servant'. He lives with his wife Mary (30), from Canterbury, his daughter Jane (2) and his father-law **William Loram** (57) from Rye, who boards with them. Ten years ago, William was living with four of his children (including Mary) and one grandchild.

The baptism record for Obediah and Mary's daughter Jane shows them living at Box Trees in 1858, and gives Obediah's occupation as 'labourer', so his position has improved significantly over the past few years.

When Obediah dies in January 1863 aged just 33, she marries James Stacey the same year. This may seem fast to us, but a widow with a young child needs a means of supporting herself.

## Two Dressmakers

**Nancy Burchett** (67) is a dressmaker and is the head of her household. She was born in Waltham and lives with her unmarried daughter Sarah (43) and a boarder **Elizabeth Bowles** (58). These women both work as dressmakers. Elizabeth is recorded as being married, but is actually a widow, having been previously married to John Burchett. Nancy passes away in 1867 and Sarah takes in the elderly Vincer sisters as boarders.

The work of a dressmaker was time-consuming and poorly paid. One of the main problems was keeping the work clean as it was worked. A dressmaker in the mid-1860s was paid less than 10s a week. However, with agricultural labourers in the area earning little more than 13s, this household was fairly affluent.

Nancy's income of 1-2 shillings per week in rent made a big difference to their lifestyle.

## Living on Bolts Hill we have:

### A Carpenter

**James Warden** (AL) (53) is married to Sarah (54) from Lyminge. Their son William (26) was born in Thanington and is now a carpenter. Their other children Ann (22), George (20) and Francis (17) were all born in Chartham and all work as agricultural labourers. This is another family that moves out of the area following a death, when Sarah dies later this year aged 55.

### The House Painter

First are **William Goodale** (61), his wife Mary (58) and their family. His occupation is Painter Master and he employs one man and one boy. Their children were all born in Chartham. The oldest sons Frederick (20) and John (13) work with their father as painters. Fanny (11), Frank (9) and granddaughter Emma (6) all go to school. James, William,

Emma, Ann, George and Victoria, who we saw on the last census, have now all left home.

It is sad to see Fanny's name in the church register. She was buried on 28th September 1866, aged 17, and even more sad to see her father's name recorded the next year. He was buried on 29th June 1867. It is no wonder the family left the area.

## A Sawyer

Next in Bolts Hill is **Stephen Cook** (65), a sawyer and his wife Sarah (67). Sarah was born in River, near Dover. Their grandson Stephen (7) was born in Chartham in 1853, to their unmarried daughter Harriet and lives with them. Harriet also gave birth to another son, William in October 1854, but he died aged 9 weeks. Sometimes between now and the next census, Stephen Snr. moves in with his son George.

## A Bricklayer

Bachelors Hall is home to **Henry Hearn** (36) an unmarried farmer's son. **Ambrose Hukins** (27), a bricklayer, boards with him. Ambrose is Thomas Hukins' son, who we first saw when he was 8, but lost sight of in the last census. He was named after his grandfather.

We see Henry on the next census, when he has finished sowing his wild oats and settled down to become a family man. He soon marries Eliza and their first child, Elizabeth, was born in 1862 while the couple still lived in Bolts Hill

## The Publican at 'The Cross Keys'

**Thomas Newington** (60) from Harbledown lives at 'The Cross Keys' and is a victualler. He lives with his wife Ann (55) who was born in Blean and no doubt helps in the pub.

Their daughter **Amelia Rudduck** (35) is living with them either permanently or is just staying with them on the night of the census while her husband is away. She has been married since 1859 and describes herself as a railway miner's wife. Amelia gives birth to her first child, Elizabeth later this year, and the child is baptized in November. The father's occupation is given as 'labourer'.

The house also houses three paying guests, widower **William Hills** (71) who boards, and is a paper maker from Loose and two unmarried lodgers: **George Broadbridge** (57) a sawyer who was born in Boughton-under-Blean and **Alfred Richardson** (31) a drover from Chilham. Alfred's job as a drover was to drive a farmer's sheep or cattle to market or to move them between fields.

This is an unusual family and it is interesting to trace their path through life to the end of the nineteenth century.

## An Engine Driver

**Thomas Cook** (36) is an engine driver, which means he is in control of a static piece of machinery, either on the farm or at the mill. He is married to Ann (40) who was born in Thanington. Their children are William (11), Mary (8) and George (6). Henry, who appeared on the 1851 census and should be aged 10 now, is missing, as he died a year after the census in 1852. They also have a boarder, **George Boorman** (28) a wheelwright from Staplehurst.

## Dealers in Wood and Cattle

**Thomas E. Dixon** (26) is a dealer in wood and was born in Selling. His wife Elizabeth (24) comes from Faversham. They do not yet have any children, although the next time we see them, they have five.

**James W. Richardson** (35) from Chilham is a dealer in cattle. He lives with his wife Ellen (29) who was born in Chartham. Their daughter Ellen (3), was born in Chilham. However, their son James (2) was born in Chartham.

# Agricultural Labourers

The following families are ones where the main wage-earner is either an agricultural labourer or a general labourer. These men were given work when the weather was good, but when the weather was poor, they were sent home without pay. This is the time that gardens and allotments were important to tide them over, along with any pennies the children earnt. The diet of the agricultural labourer, always underpinned by the hedgerow harvest around them, was even more reliant on what was gathered in the fields and hedgerows.

## A Nurse

**Anny Philpott** (47) a nurse/domestic from Fordwich is the head of her household now her husband William has passed away. She lives with her children Amelia (9), Charles (7) and James (4). She supplements her income by having two boarders, **Eliza Friar** (35) who works as a dressmaker and describes herself as married, with her son James (16) (AL). Only Anny was born outside of Chartham.

The period after harvest was particularly busy for Eliza, as people were paid and be in need of warm clothes to keep them going through the winter.

The two women will be glad of the company and Eliza will be able to help Anny with the younger children, especially with her dressmaking skills to help supplement those of Anny as James moves from his baby skirts into knickerbockers.,

# Shalmsford Street

Vincer Cottage

## Uncle William Boards with Them

**John Browning** (48) (AL) is from Waltham and has a member of the family staying with him as a paying guest. His wife Mary (39) from Chilham works as an agricultural labourer and her brother **Williams Hulks (Hulse?)** (64) (AL) lives with them as a boarder. Mary and John have one son, also called John (3). The family soon move to Underdown, where they live for several decades.

## Charles Gets a Home of His Own

The next household is that of **Charles (Ruck) Vincer** (30) (AL) and his wife Eliza (28). Their children are Stephen (5) and Jane (2). The whole family were born in Chartham, where Stephen goes to school. Charles was previously living with his mother, Elizabeth Vincer, and continues to live in the area for the rest of the century. We will see Charles' family grow as we trace his records.

## Three Sisters

**Elizabeth Vincer** (52) lives with her siblings, sisters Maria (43) and Esther (39), and is mother to Charles Vincer, who also lives in the village. Their niece Eliza (15), from Bridge, lives with them and although she is listed as scholar, and keeps house while all three are working as agricultural labourers. She may also be employed at the school as a pupil teacher to help the schoolmaster.

The parish records show the baptism of Anne Maria Vincer in July 1863. The mother is recorded as being Maria Vincer, spinster, of Shalmsford Street.

I found the name Vincer again on the records for 1869. This time Eliza has given birth to a daughter, Maria Elizabeth, baptized in March.

Lastly, the name Vincer also appears on the burial records, when Elizabeth is buried on 18th August 1861, aged 53.

## Helping at the School

**Stephen Wenham** (40) (AL) and his wife Maria (35) are next. Their daughter Martha (13) is listed as a scholar and due to her age, she may be paying her way through school by working as a pupil teacher. The couple move to Faversham before the next census and Martha marries Daniel Miller in Elham.

## This Family is Still Growing

**Henry Spillett** (42) (AL) lives with Phoebe (nee Hogben) (35) his wife. Their son John (14) works with his parents as an agricultural labourer. Henry (9) goes to school while George (4) and Edwin (1) stay at home, looked after by Henry or looked in on by the neighbours. The family are still in Shalmsford Street in 1871, although Phoebe passed away in 1870, having borne three more children.

## A Comfortable Household

**James Austen** (50) married Elizabeth Hoare (45) from Chartham in 1833. They and their four eldest children Ellen (19), James (17), Charlotte (13) and Edward (11) all work as agricultural labourers. The two youngest, Emily (9) and Jesse (3) are listed as scholars. We can follow this family as they stay in Shalmsford Street.

The village school at the bottom of Bolts Hill, now a doctor's surgery, was not built until the early 1870s, so children attended a National School in Chartham. The Old School House was on Chartham Village Green, almost opposite the forge.

## A Loyal Member

Next are **George Hoare** (58) and his wife Mary (56) who was born in Challock. They work as agricultural labourers, as does their daughter Sarah (20). Their son Jesse is 18 and is learning to make and mend shoes as a cordwainer's apprentice. Their boarder is **James Rye** (21), a bricklayers labourer from Ickham. This is the last time we see Jesse with his family, as he is married by the time of the 1871 census.

It is interesting to note that George was awarded £1 on 25 Nov 1862 by the Chartham Agricultural Association for 33 years membership of a benefit society, namely the Prince of Orange Benefit Society. I believe this was a benefit society called The United Kentish Britons that met at The Prince of Orange pub in Orange Street, Canterbury. It was run by subscription "for raising a fund to afford relief to its members in case of sickness or infirmity". These funds acted as a kind of health insurance.

## A Family That's Going Places

Henry's uncle, **Stephen Spillett** (43) (AL) and his family are in the next household. His wife Caroline is now 38 and their children are Ester (15), Martha (11), Edwin (7) and Sophia (5). Martha and Edwin are the only children who go to school, while Ester has left to become a domestic servant. The family move out of the area and by 1871 to live in Chartham Hatch.

## A Household of Women

**William Friars** (47) is head of the next household, consisting of just him and his wife Sarah, who is the same age. Their daughter Eliza is 22. All three work as agricultural labourers.

## Yes, Miss

Another **Henry Spillett,** Stephen's brother, (32) (AL) lives with his wife Sophia (28) who is a schoolmistress at the Day School. In 1851, Henry was listed as lodging with the Philpotts. The couple never have children of their own, and eventually adopt.

## Making Ends Meet

**George Spillett** (27) (AL), another of Stephen's nephews, also married a girl from Petham, Harriett Jarvis (30). They have two sons, John (3) and George (1). They have one boarder, **Henry Hulse** (23) who also works on the land. We can watch this family as their family grow and they stay in the area. George is brother to Henry Spillett.

## Two Boys for Ann

**William Fisher** (43) (AL) has moved here from Newington near Hythe. His wife Ann (31) was Ann Link before her marriage, and we are able to follow their history through the years, until Ann moves into widowhood. Their children James (5) and John (1) were born in Chartham. At age five, James still attends school, but, given his father's occupation, I cannot but think that this will be a short-lived duty.

## Labouring in the Fields and Building Sites

**George Cork** (44) is a bricklayer's labourer. His wife Elizabeth from Waltham is a little older than him at 49 and she works as an agricultural labourer. Their sons Henry (13) and William (10) were both born in Chartham, and although there is no job title listed for the boys, they certainly were not idle. A boy of this age could earn half to two-thirds of the salary of a grown man, which made a huge difference to the family's budget. Daughters Charlotte, Sarah and Amy have left home. This whole family stay in Shalmsford.

Next is his brother **Henry Cork** (34) also a bricklayer's labourer with a wife from Waltham. His wife is called Jane and she works as an agricultural labourer. Their children are Charlotte (11), Eliza (8), Emily (5), George (3) and Sarah (7 months). Henry and Jane earn enough money between them to be able to send both Charlotte and Eliza to school.

Another member of the Cork family, Edward, is born on January 1864. He is swiftly followed by his twin William, who dies three weeks later.

Just because the Cork brothers are listed next to each other in the enumerator's book does not necessarily mean that they live next door to each other, as the return papers were copied by the enumerator into the book, so they were not in the same order as the houses in the street. If someone was not at home, the enumerators had to collect it another day, putting the returns out of order.

Eliza dies in the autumn of 1864 and is buried on 25th September.

## An Unusual Name

Next are **Archley Harlow** (25) (AL) and his wife Ellen who is the same age. Their children are Phoebe (5), Emma (3) and George (6 months). The whole family was born in Chartham.

Archley and Emma have another child in 1863. Their daughter Rachel is baptized on June 28th at St Marys, Chartham, and the couple give Shalmsford Street as their address. Rachel must be a family name, as John and Charlotte Harlow name their daughter Rachel in 1860.

The family move to Chilham in 1869-70, which we can date accurately due to the birth places of their children. Thomas is born in Chartham in September 1868, and the next child is born in the summer of 1870. One name that will be missing from the list is that of little George, who dies in 1873 and is buried on March 10th.

## Elizabeth Stays with Nanny

**Thomas Wraight** (63) (AL) from Harbledown lives next, with his wife Charlotte (52) from Wye. Their daughter Sarah is 26 is unmarried and works as a domestic servant. Thomas' granddaughter Elizabeth Wraight (2) is also shown as living in the house. Look out for this family on successive census returns as their family grows.

Thomas passes away in 1869 and is buried on 27th February of that year.

## Enjoying Retirement

**Thomas Homersham** (75) and his wife Charlotte (65) are both now retired. Thomas was born in Canterbury and Charlotte was born in Tuppington.

## Brother and Sister

Stephen Spickett, husband to **Sarah Spickett** (56), who we met in 1841, has died and she never re-marries. She now lives with her widowed brother **John Marsh** (42) and his daughter Ann (14). All three are agricultural labourers. **Emily Russell** (10) is recorded as a boarder in their house, but no mention is made of any family connection, so it is unclear on what basis this has happened. She is listed as a scholar, so she attends the local school.

## Who Looks After Thomas?

**William Philpott** (52) lives with his wife Harriet (46) and they are also agricultural labourers. Their daughters Jane (12) and Hannah (9) and their son Thomas (6) are still at home. The girls are listed as scholars, but Thomas is not, even though he is only six. The girls might be acting as pupil teachers.

Next door, **William Hayward** (75) and his wife Thomazin (68) both work as agricultural labourers. Thomas was born in Wye and Thomazin in Kennington, near Ashford. Having lived a long life, Thomazin dies in 1869, and William moves away.

## Twin Trouble

**James Link** (55) lives with his wife Jane (51) and their children James (33), Henry (15), twins William (9) and Jane (9), and George (13). Young George is an agricultural labourer like his parents, and James Jnr is a carter's mate.

A large family like this will have benefitted hugely from the income generated by its various members. The census returns record only the occupation of the adults, and usually only that of the men in the house, but the casual labour of the women and children made a big difference to the standard of living within the household.

A report of 1870 shows that children were employed in shaving hop poles and cutting sticks in January, sowing beans and peas in the early spring, and planting potatoes in the late spring. Early summer was a time for weeding, bird scaring and haymaking, leading to the thinning and harvesting of crops in late summer. After working with the adults during the harvest in August, they were required to look after the pigs and sheep as they grazed the stubble fields. Potatoes were harvested in October after which came two months of winter work, muck spreading, stone picking, collecting acorns for the pigs and tending the winter corn. All these jobs were paid at a fraction of the wages earnt by adult workers.

## Left Holding the Baby

**John Link** is a 27-year-old agricultural labourer, and is son to William and Hannah. His wife Mary Ann is a year younger than John and was born in London. Their sons William (10) and James (4) were born in St Mildreds, Canterbury, but the youngest son, Edward (1) was born in Chartham. This family is one of the longest-standing in Shalmsford and we see members come and go. Mary is the one we lose this time, as she dies in 1862, aged 31, possibly due to complications after the birth of her next child. The discrepancy in her age could either be due to a genuine mistake or it could be a deliberate error.

## A Match Made in Heaven

**John Link** (25) lives with Ann (nee Mongeham) (44), his wife. He is a boot and shoe maker and one of James and Jane's children. This little family are obviously a love match and their numbers grow over the years. Ann gives birth to a daughter later this year; Emily is baptized in Chartham in October 1851.

## The Children Leave Home

**William Baker** (61) (AL) lives with his wife Eliza (52) and his much-reduced family. His daughter Eliza (21) works as a servant and Jane (12) and William (7) are scholars. Mary, Charlotte, Henry and William have left home. George, William's grandson is only 5 months old and appears on the census along with Frances his granddaughter who is 3 months old. Frances' mother is Eliza and William's mother is Charlotte, who may just be absent on the night of the census as she and her son are seen living with the family in 1871.

I also have found a baptism record for George, son of Charlotte Baker in November 1860. This could be another grandson for William.

## A Grandson for Richard

**Richard Hoare** (56) lives next with his wife Elizabeth (49) who have three children still at home. Two, James (22) and Phoebe (20) work as agricultural labourers like their parents, while Jesse (18) is a carter's mate. Also in the house is their grandson **William Cook** (3) who was born in Bridge. John, Sarah Jane and Ann have moved away, while Frances and Harriet have died.

## Living with Their Grandparents

**Joseph Washford** (70) lives with his wife Sarah (68) and their grandson **Joseph Andrews** (16) and all three work as agricultural labourers. Joseph was born in Kingsnorth, Sarah in Loose and Joseph in Chartham. **James Goodale** (6) is another grandson who lives with them; he is Harriot's son. Like other families in the village, they supplement their income by taking in a boarder. **George Somerford** (19) is a baker's journeyman from Fordwich, who boards with them. George wore an off-white jacket, yellow waistcoat and a flat tam-o'-shanter style white hat.

Joseph dies in 1869 before the next census, but Sarah continues to live in the area with James.

## Living with Grandpa

**George Burchett** (76) still works as an agricultural labourer, despite his age. He still lives with his son George (50), a shoemaker, and daughter-in-law Mary (53). Also in the house is George Jnr's child Ambrose (8) who goes to school. There are two George Burchetts in Shalmsford at this time, a labourer and a bricklayer, so it is hard to unravel which is which, especially as they all seem to have married women called Mary. George Snr dies in 1867 aged 81.

## On his Own but not Lonely

**John Young** (41) is a carter who was born in Chilham. He lives on his own, which he continues to do for the rest of his long life in Shalmsford.

### A Baby in the House

**John Barker** (60) works as an agricultural labourer, as do his daughter Ann (22) and his son John (15). Also in the house is John's grandson, Stephen Barker, 8 months old, who is Ann's illegitimate son. **Charlotte Hulks (Hulse?)** (22) is a visitor to the house. Her occupation is given as 'servant', although she is not the servant in this house, as she wouldn't be noted as a visitor. Was she looking after the baby? After John's death in 1864, the family move out of the area.

### An Independent Woman

**Lydia Sacree**, a 64-year-old retiree from Petham lives on her own in the next house and stays in Shalmsford until her death in 1874.

### Little Sarah Keeps them Young

**Henry Banks** (63) and his wife Sarah (60), from Hardres, are both agricultural labourers. Their granddaughter, also called Sarah who is aged three, lives with them. Henry dies later this year, and is buried in St Mary's churchyard, after which the family move out of the area.

## Bolts Hill

### Six Children and Room for a Lodger

**William Gipson** (33) is a bricklayer's labourer and lives with his wife Sarah (33) from Devon. Their children were all born in Chartham. Unlike the more affluent families, the children have been sent out to work at an early age; George (13) and Frances(11) are both agricultural labourers. Only the next daughter Rosa (6) is at school. The younger ones are Jesse (4) Liley (2) and John William (2 months). This large family has also taken in a boarder – widower **Henry Cook** (65) still works as an agricultural labourer.

### Family Nearby

**Richard Gipson** (70), who we met in 1841, is still an agricultural labourer and is married to Elizabeth (66) from Petham. The church records show the burial of Elizabeth Gipson of Bolts Hill on 19th September 1868, and in 1871 Richard Jipson is shown lodging in Chartham Village.

Next are **John Gipson** (52) and his wife Sarah (51) from Sittingbourne with their son Joseph (20). Their lodger is **Henry Wright** (24) from Moldash, a local variation of the village name Molash. All four work as agricultural labourers. John dies in 1863 and Sarah remarries. This couple are the parents of John Gipson, who has married Harriet Hoare and now live in Rattington Street, Chartham, before moving into Shalmsford Street in the 1870s.

### A Growing Brood

**George Andreas** (30) (AL) is from St Stephens (Canterbury). His wife Mary (21) comes from nearby Waltham. They have one son, George (7 months) who was born in Chartham. They do not stay long in this area.

## Happy Together

**William Cozens** (AL) and his wife Sarah are both 77. They live in a small household of two. Sarah dies in 1866 and William follows her in 1870

## Deanery Cottages

**Thomas Livermore** (55) lives in one of the two Deanery Cottages with his wife Jane (45). They are both agricultural labourers. Thomas was born in Felsted and Jane in Stebbing. They have one boarder, **James Smith** (19) a carter's mate from Great Leighs in Essex. This is another group of people that we do not see again.

A quick mention should be made of the dangers of seeing the census information as an indication of long-term residency. Time and again I have seen newspaper reports and adverts telling us about people who never appear on the census returns, as they move in and out of the area through the decade.

One such piece of information is the notice in The Kentish Gazette dated November 3rd 1868. Mr E. Robinson is moving out of the area and is selling his household furniture and shop fittings. He has been living in Shalmsford Street and making a living as a boot and shoe maker, but is now leaving. Due to the problems associated with transportation of large items, he has decided to sell everything before starting again in a new area. The items in the auction include a French iron bedstead, mattress, wash and dressing tables, dressing glasses, chest of drawers, bed-room carpets, chairs, fenders, fire irons etc., etc., six and one elbow mahogany cane set chairs, easy chair in leather, chimney glass, mahogany couch in hair cloth, loo, and Pembroke tables, American clock, French clock and shade, kitchen requisites, and sundry articles of earthenware etc. Also shop counter, shelves, shoe lasts, specks, sundry tools and a variety of useful articles.

We also see that Herbert Wills appears on the 1867 Register of Electors, but he is not living in Shalmsford Street at the time of the 1861 census. He moves on fairly quickly, as he does not appear on the 1871 census either. It is interesting that his address is given as 'Shalmsford Street', while other voters, who we know live in the area, are listed under 'Chartham'.

## Other Records

The baptism and burial records of St Mary's church also give clues as to the number of people living in the village who are not recorded on the census:

- Mary Wright, who was buried on 29th April 1860 aged 50.

- Thomas Fox who was buried on 27th March 1860, aged 89.

- Jane Wright aged 53 who died in 1862.

- The Cork family lose people in this decade, as they did in the last, with Mary Ann of Bolts Hill dying in 1863 aged 69.

- Rosetta Gould is recorded in the parish records as having lived in Shalmsford Street. She was buried on 12th August 1963 aged 12.

- Fanny Spillet was born 1 April 1863 and buried in September, but I cannot find the names of her parents. There is no birth record for her in the parish archives.

- Charlotte Dale was living in Bolts Hill at the time of her death in 1867. She was 47.

- Jameson Hayward was living in Shalmsford Street when he died in April 1868 aged 75.

- Charles Baker was living in the same street in 1869 when he passed away aged 39.

- John, son of John and Charlotte Harlow died in 1862 aged 3 weeks.

The average cost of a funeral about this time was £5. As the average annual wage was only about £25 per annum, many families paid a weekly sum into a funeral fund to pay for this.

- But some new faces have also appeared in the village.

- Ellen Eliza was born to John and Maria Goldup. John was a shoemaker and the family lived in Shalmsford Street.

- John and Mary Browning welcome baby George into their family in 1862.-

- George and Charlotte Spillett welcome Frederick John in 1862. This couple appeared on the last census, but for some reason have not filled in an 1861 return. George is another son to Thomas who lives in Long Neck Punchgate Cottage.

- George and Harriet Cork's baby Richard George is baptized in December 1862.

- We saw James Mitchell Hoare and his wife Emma in the 1851 census, but they are absent in this one and in 1871. They do, however, appear on the church records, giving an address of Shalmsford Street in 1863 at the baptism of their baby Ann, for the baptism of baby Fanny in 1864, and again in 1866 when baby Mitchell is baptized and dies aged 7 weeks. The couple have another baby in 1867, Alfred.

- Herbert and Elizabeth Stockbridge live long enough in the village to list Shalmsford Street as their address at the baptism of their baby William Herbert in July 1868.

- The same is true for George and Martha Emery, whose baby Stephen was baptised in August 1868.

- Henry James Harlow and his wife Eliza welcome baby William in January 1869. Henry gives his occupation as 'farmer'.

- Baby Harriett Maria is born to George and Ann Sims in February 1869 and Michael and Fanny Sims welcome baby John in the same year.

- Alfred is born to Joseph and Louisa Ann Collard in 1869 also of Shalmsford Street.

- William of born to George and Caroline Tappenden the same year.

Box Trees House

# The 1870s

The 1870s were a time of expansion for the little village of Shalmsford, as it inched further towards becoming synonymous with the village of Chartham. Two main building projects affected Shalmsford Street. Firstly, the construction of a new Primitive Methodist Chapel, opened in 1874, which was replaced by the current building in 1906. The church was closed in the early 2000s and it is now being used as two residential properties.

Secondly, the St Augustine's asylum was opened in 1875 as a self-contained residential area. The building of the asylum provided work for many people in the area, bringing a degree of prosperity. Once it was completed, it also offered occupation, firstly for people who lived on site, and gradually for families who lived in Shalmsford and travelled up the hill to work each day. The 120-acre site was taken over by the NHS in 1948 and eventually closed in 1993.

The 1870s were a wet decade, with 1875 and 1876 being noted for the amount of mildewed crops, and 1879 being particularly wet during the summer. The harvest was slow to ripen, and late to be gathered in. 1877 was the year the potato crop failed, and in 1879 farmers had to face liver rot in sheep and pleuro-pneumonia in their cattle. This was the decade that was to become known as an agricultural depression. The problem was so widespread and so bad that many look to this as the beginning of the decline in English agriculture.

Another important change to note since the last census is that the Education Act of 1870 is now in force. All children between the ages of 5 and 10 are required to attend school on a daily basis, and it is the parents' duty to ensure that they attend. The new schools are financed jointly by the church and the village. Previously, the only schooling many children received was from the Sunday Schools, which were run by churches for the benefit of the poor. Unlike modern Sunday Schools, pupils were offered up to eight hours of tuition and stayed at school for the whole day. At the beginning of Victoria's reign, only eleven elementary schools had existed in Kent, the nearest to Shalmsford being in Petham.

Chartham Primary School opened in October 1872, under the guidance of Anthony Martin, Certified Teacher 2nd class, and a certified schoolmistress was employed to oversee a team of 'pupil teachers' who were the older children working much as Teaching Assistants do today, ensuring that the group under their supervision completed the tasks set by the teacher. Many went on to become teachers themselves, and were paid a nominal wage which amounted to little more than pocket money, but still gave a working class child a chance to move up the social ladder. During the first months, the school accommodated approximately 60 pupils per day, although the logbook at the end of the first week records that

*'The children have evidently no previous discipline worth mentioning. Their notions of what school habits should be are of the loosest description.'*

A few pennies a week was charged for the schooling, although this was waived for the poorest families. The agreed fees were 3d for the first child, 2d for the second and 1d for the third and subsequent children. Children who lived locally went home for dinner at what we now call lunchtime, while those who travelled some distance were allowed to bring dinner with them.

By November, the teacher recorded in the ledger that

*'Some of the books have already begun to suffer from the absence of a lavatory at the school.'*

I gather from this that children were relieving themselves outside and using pages from the books as toilet paper.

The committee had agreed to continue the school as a National School, overseen by the church, but after it ran into financial difficulties, they agreed to register as a Board School, by which means they were entitled to government funding. The registration was completed in the summer of 1874. One of their first decisions was to reduce the school fee to one penny per child per week.

The school is clearly located in a rural area, and as we have heard, the income from child labour was an important part of each family's budget. This is demonstrated in the school logbook, which records absences at hop tying, fruit picking and other harvesting times.

This was the decade that the Poor Laws were changed. Districts were divided into administrative districts called Unions, and Shalmsford came within the Bridge Union. Up until now, any person requiring relief had to be admitted to a workhouse. After 1871, people in need were able to apply for 'outdoor relief', that is, they were granted money without entering the workhouse.

The telegraph was introduced a year before the census, in 1870, and I wonder how many people in Shalmsford received one. I suspect it was very few.

Another innovation introduced in 1871 was the allowance of Bank Holidays to working people. Previously to this, Good Friday and Christmas Day was the only days of rest, apart from Sundays. The Bank Holiday Act allowed a holiday on Easter Monday, Whit Monday, the first Monday in August and Boxing Day, bringing the total allowance to six days a year.

1874 saw the repeal of sugar duties, making sugar a much more affordable commodity. This can be seen as one of the major turning points in the lowering of British health, as it suddenly became part of the diets of many people who had previously been unable to afford it. This lowering of tax meant that commercially produced jam now became widely available (Harley's was started in 1871) and confectionary and sweet shops became viable.

The parents whose children hanker to join the military will have been pleased by the siting of a new barracks for The Buffs just outside Canterbury, and even more pleased to learn that the option of discharge is now being offered after six years instead of the previous twenty-one. All soldiers in the regiments are now to be issued with breach-loading rifles.

This was the decade that Shalmsford asserted its Methodist ideals. The Wesleyan Methodist chapel was built at the bottom of Bolts Hill. It is now a residential property, but still retains the name La Chapelle. In 1879 and the Primitive Methodist Chapel was built in 1874.

Up until now, I have relied on Church of England baptismal records for information regarding new arrivals in Shalmsford. After 1875, it was a legal requirement that the birth of a baby was recorded in a civil register. It is an odd fact to note that the birth rate began to fall in the 1870s, after a period in which families became smaller, dropping from the usual 6-8 children, and that this phenomenon continued across all classes. Illegitimacy rates also fell from this date onwards, on into the twentieth century, and although many records have been lost or supressed, evidence can still be found in the records of the local workhouse.

## 1871 Census

The 1871 census recorded where people stayed on the night of 2nd April. The Shalmsford Street/Bolts Hill area has now grown to house 83 households.

Once again, the census enumerator was George Baker Ruff who continues to farm in Rattington Street and has extended his acreage from 119 to 164 acres on his dairy farm Enumeration District 2 was described as 'Part of the parish of Chartham situated on the south side of the River Stour, including Perry Farm, Thruxted Farm, Underdown Cottages, Mystole House, Long Neck, Pickleden, Shalmsford Street, Bolts Hill, Chartham Deanery, Court Lodge, Rattington Street, Horton Chapel Farm and Cottages, Downs Farm, Parish Road and the Boxtrees.'

The range of ages in the village has now skewed slightly in favour of the older generation. There are now 95 under-10s and 23 70-80 year olds. The number of under-10s has only increased by 25% whereas the number of older people has doubled. However, this changes dramatically in 1881.

## Trades and Professions

The number and scope of those undertaking definable trades and professions has once again grown. The list of trades in Shalmsford in 1871 is as follows:

Occupations in Shalmsford, 1871

| | | |
|---|---|---|
| Agricultural labourer | 42 | 32% |
| Labourer | 13 | 10% |
| Domestic servant | 10 | 8% |
| Carpenter | 5 | 4% |
| Paper mill worker | 5 | 4% |
| Apprentice to trade | 3 | 2% |
| Farmer | 3 | 2% |
| Paper sorter | 3 | 2% |
| Woodsman | 3 | 2% |
| Baker | 2 | 1% |
| Bricklayer | 2 | 1% |
| Dressmaker/seamstress | 2 | 1% |
| Engine driver | 2 | 1% |
| Factory girl/boy | 2 | 1% |
| Gardener | 2 | 1% |
| Grocer | 2 | 1% |
| Housekeeper | 2 | 1% |
| Paper maker | 2 | 1% |
| Paper mill glazier | 2 | 1% |
| Paper mill rag cutter | 2 | 1% |
| School mistress | 2 | 1% |
| Bavin maker | 1 | <1% |
| Blacksmith | 1 | <1% |
| Boot and shoe maker | 1 | <1% |
| Brickmaker | 1 | <1% |
| Builder | 1 | <1% |
| Coal merchant | 1 | <1% |
| Dealer | 1 | <1% |
| Farm servant | 1 | <1% |
| Horticulturalist | 1 | <1% |
| House decorator/plumber | 1 | <1% |
| Laundress | 1 | <1% |
| Licenced victualler | 1 | <1% |
| Nurse | 1 | <1% |
| Paper bleacher | 1 | <1% |
| Policeman | 1 | <1% |
| Painter | 1 | <1% |
| Publican | 1 | <1% |
| Soldier | 1 | <1% |
| Wheelwright | 1 | <1% |
| Blacksmith | 1 | <1% |
| | | |
| TOTAL | 131 | |

As before, I start with families in which the main breadwinner works in an identifiable trade or profession.

## Shalmsford Street

### A Laundress

Firstly, our friend **John Link** (36) the boot and shoe maker and his wife Ann (54), who is a laundress, who have only one child at home: Emily (9).

Washing from neighbouring families who were not in possession of a boiler or mangle was brought to the laundress on a Friday, soaked on Saturday and washed on Monday. It was returned to their owners starched, folded and sometimes ironed, as soon as it was dry. Emily, at age nine was the ideal age to help, neither too young to be strong enough nor old enough to have a job of her own.

It is interesting to speculate on where the water for household us came from, as well as the vast amounts needed for laundering. Many houses had wells in the back gardens, and water could have been collected directly from the river. There was also a pump outside number 63, and I wonder if it was a communal pump for the use of those who had no other access to fresh water.

I have been told that the row of cottages called Park View Terrace, next to The Primitive Methodist Church had two 'set pot' boilers to share between the six houses. The cottages had two wells behind them, which were filled in during the 1960s. These cottages were built in 1850, and this could well have been the workplace of Ann Pay.

## A Brickmaker

Brickfield Cottage is home to **Richard Jones** (33) a brickmaker, his wife Emily (31), and seven children: Margarette (15) a rag cutter, working at the paper mill, Hannah (11), Mary (10), William (9), Sarah (7), Richard (5), Jane (2). Richard dies in 1874 and Emily remarries, joining her family with that of her new husband, making a total of 11 children in one household. This cottage is possibly on the site of Irfon Cottage, which is adjacent to a brickfield.

A very interesting article can be found at www.benfleethistory.org.uk where the process of preparing and firing bricks using a clamp instead of a kiln is described. As I have found no evidence of kilns in the Shalmsford area, it seems likely they were using clamps to fire the bricks. This was a slower process, but just as effective. Details of the brickmaking process in Sittingbourne can be seen at miltoncreekmemories.co.uk/bricks/, which I expect is very similar to the brickmaking in Shalmsford, although on a larger scale.

## An Engine Driver

**Henry Cook**, (40) is an engine driver, and his wife Charlotte (33) looks after their children Alfred (4) and Albert (7 months). The couple stay in the village and have more children, but towards the end of his life, Henry takes on less strenuous jobs.

## A Grocer

**John Homersham** (57) is a grocer and coal merchant employing one man; his shop is by the railway bridge. His wife Elizabeth (57) helps with the business and his son George (24) also works as an assistant. Their daughter Maryann (22) is unmarried. The family previously had a servant living with them. They either now have a 'daily woman' or have no need for a servant while Maryann is living with them. John also rents two pieces of arable land near the entrance to Chartham Deanery as a yearly tenant.

This is the last census where John has control of the business; by 1881 George has taken over and allows him to retire. George Homersham is also the enumerator for the 1881 census, which is a fitting transfer of duties.

John Homersham rents several pieces of land in the area, as shown on an advert of land for sale in December 1871. He is noted as the tenant of an acre of 'excellent' arable land near the entrance to The Deanery, and just over five acres of 'very productive' arable land behind the Hop Oast opposite The Deanery.

John rents the house and shop where he lives and works, and this property comes up for sale in 1873. The local paper gives details, telling us of the nine rooms, stables, stores, cart-shed and a good walled garden. It is of interest to note that Mr J. Homerhsam is listed as a draper. It could be that this was part of his business, run by his wife. I know that Park House, now demolished, consisted of several of these elements, and added to the fact that the land on which it stood is still surrounded by a substantial walled garden, I suspect that this was John's home. He also rented adjoining pasture-land.

We see on the 1881 census that he is listed as a retired grocer.

One of the activities her pursued during his retirement was pursuing activities as a member of the School Management Committee, to which he was elected in 1872.

## A Baker

**William D. Matthews** (25) a journeyman baker, was lodging with the Shrubsole family in 1871, but now has a wife and two children. He lives with Harriot (26), and his young family: Harriot (7) and Esther (3).

## Three Gardeners

**Thomas Read** (32) is a gardener, which pays enough to provide a home for Rebecca (32), Arthur (5), Minnie (3) and Albert (2). He would be spotted about the village wearing trousers, a waistcoat, and of course the trade-mark blue apron. The couple soon move back to Quainton, Bucks, where they were both born, taking their family with them.

Rebecca gives birth to another son this year. Fred is baptized on June 27th, but they have to say goodbye to him when he dies aged just 1 month. He is buried in Chartham churchyard. Perhaps this is why they moved away from the area.

**Henry Hayward** (54) is also a gardener and lives with his son William (19) who works at the paper mill as a paper maker. Charles (17) is a printer. Also in the house are his granddaughter Fanny (9) scholar, Edward his son (28) a labourer, Roseina (22), his daughter and granddaughter

Roseina (1), I suspect that Edward and Roseina are married to each other and Roseina is in fact Henry's daughter-in-law. This would mean that Fanny is the daughter of a different son.

The Whitstable Times and Herne Bay Herald dated 10th June 1871 reports on the Annual Fete of the United Britons Benefit Society, which 'caused Shalmsford Street to be more lively than on any other day in the year'. It was 'ably conducted' by Henry Hayward, who has managed it for the last nineteen years. The article reports that the club has been in existence for 30-40 years, and that 150 members came together for dinner at 'The George' at 2pm.

**Joseph Stubberfield** (58), horticulturist, lives with his wife Harriott (57) and their daughter Mary Ann (28) who is unmarried and indeed never does marry. Harriott was missing from the 1861 census return, but she must have been visiting a friend or relative, for she is now returned to the family home.

The local paper of 1873 tells us that Joseph is living in one of a pair of brick and tile semi-detached cottages, which are listed as adjacent to The Old Bakery; this would mean that the two cottages are now numbers 43 and 45 Shalmsford Street. He rents both and sub-lets one. He also rents pasture land further along Shalmsford Street.

## A Wheelwright ...

**William Bangham** (33) a wheelwright lives with his wife May Ann (30), and their children William Henry (10), Henry William (4). **John Hogben** (23) is a boarder in the house. He works as a labourer. They have moved here from Harvey's Row in Chartham, but choose to stay in Shalmsford.

## ... and Four Carpenters

**William Chambers** (40) is a carpenter and lives with his wife Lucy (34). The also share their home with **Alfred Smith,** a boarder aged six. Later this year Lucy gives birth to William James, who is baptized on July 2nd. William and Lucy soon leave Shalmsford and move into Church Lane, Chartham.

**James Pay** (60), a carpenter, and Ann (60) live on their own now their children have left home. James dies in 1873, leaving less than £100.

I found a baptism record for a baby Elizabeth Pay, born to Sarah Pay of Shalmsford Street in January 1873, and I think she is James and Ann's granddaughter, and that Sarah has come home to have the baby after working as a servant in Ashford. Sadly, the baby dies at 11 weeks old.

**Charles Ruck** (66) the carpenter still lives with his wife Matilda (55) and **Amelia Long** (53), Matilda's sister, is still living with them, but all the children have now left home.

**William Ruck** (31) is a qualified (journeyman) carpenter. His household consists of himself, Maria (nee Brown) (35), William (10), Livania (5) and Benjamin (1). William had been living with his parents, Charles and Matilda, in 1861. He has named his daughter after his favourite sister. The family stay in the village and prosper.

William and Maria's next child, Lucy Sophia was born in 1872, but she dies in 1874.

A notice in the local newspaper gives details of four brick and slate cottages for sale. They are listed as being in the occupation of Messrs. Lawler, Ruck, Burchett and Cook, and are adjacent to John Homersham's shop, and are therefore numbers 81-83 Shalmsford Street, previously known as Fern Cottages. These four cottages were sold while the tenants remained in possession. Although I cannot be sure, as there are several families with these surnames, it is logical to assume that Henry Cook and William Ruck are two of the occupants.

## Two Bricklayers

**John Adams** (72) the bricklayer is married to Mary (72). Mary dies in 1878, and John moves in with his son and stays in Shalmsford Street.

**Tritton Adams** (46), bricklayer, and his wife Rebecca (46) now live with their children Robert (13), Harriott (11), Alfred (9), William (7) and James (3) as well as **John Hearn** (AL) (60) Rebecca's widowed father. Harriot marries James Link before the next census and has her first child in 1881. Tritton has now dropped his first name (James) and is known as Tritton.

## A Farmer for Shalmsford Street

**John Gambrill** (46) farmer of 155 acres employing 4 men and 2 boys, lives at Shalmsford Farm, having taken over from his father, Joseph. His wife is Catherine (40), and their large household includes their four children Flora (13), Harriott Mary (6), Sydney (4) and Sarah (1). **Mary Allen** (63) is Catherine's widowed mother and was formerly a butcher's wife. They have two indoor servants, **Edward Arnold** (26) and **William Harris** (17).

## Single Again

**Philip Hukins** (71), formerly a bricklayer, is now a widower and lives on his own since the death of his wife. Philip dies in 1876.

## Dressmaking at Home

The unmarried **Sarah Ann Burchill** (53) supports herself by working as a dressmaker. She also has an income from taking in boarders. Her two boarders are **Maria Vincer** (56) and her daughter Ann Vincer (8). I can find no mention of Sarah after this census.

As manufactured clothing was now cheaper and more available, Sarah was reduced to undertaking the more basic sewing and mending tasks. Since the introduction of the railways, second-hand clothing was now another option for the cash-strapped agricultural worker and his family.

## The Grocer

Our friend **Phineas Shrubsole** (78) is still the local baker and grocer. He and his wife Esther (72) never had children. **Sophia Harris** (29) is a general domestic servant lives who with them. William has left.

In 1873, the bakery is offered for sale, giving the details as comprising six rooms, shop, kitchen and offices, detached bakehouse with oven and stove and an acre of garden and orchard. Having lived a long life together, during which the lack of children may have made them even closer, Esther dies in 1876 and Phineas follows her in 1877.

## The Publican at 'The George'

At 'The George' we have **George Webb** (41) licenced victualler with his wife Frances (40), **Emma Hopper** his niece (11) and three boarders, **Henry Lee** (40) (AL) is a widower and presumably father to Henry Lee boarder (12) **Richard Pay** unmarried (35) (AL) is also a boarder and the last member of this household.

Four years earlier, 'The George' had been under the management of Thomas Streeting, as recorded in The Whitstable Times:

From the Whitstable Times and Herne Bay Herald,

*Saturday 12 January, 1867. Price 1d.*

*CHARTHAM. GAMBLING.*

*At the County Police Court, on Saturday Thomas Newington, landlord of "'The Cross Keys'," and Robert Streeting, of 'The George', both in this parish, pleaded guilty to allowing raffling to be carried on in their houses during the Christmas holidays, and were each fined 1 shilling. costs 10 shillings.*

This may be the incident which caused him to give up the trade and pass it on to George Webb. By 1871, Mr and Mrs Webb have made the pub a centre of the local community, as shown by another report in The Whitstable Times and Herne Bay Herald from 1871, which reports on the annual fete (see above) for which they provided 'a substantial dinner in their well-known and excellent style'.

George Webb leaves 'The George' in 1879 and Stephen Goldup takes over again for a few of years before James Stupples moves in.

Visitors to both 'The Cross Keys' and 'The George' were been able to enjoy a pint of locally-brewed beer, perhaps listen to someone reading aloud from the newspaper, discuss affairs of the day and engage in a game of dominoes, darts or skittles. The pub closed at 10pm, although opening times were variable and often early.

## One Shoemaker

**George Birchett** (60) is a boot and shoe maker He lives with his wife Mary (63) and their son Ambrose (18) in an area called 'loam pits'. Listed next in the enumerator's book is Sarah Birchett (74) seamstress living in 'a lean-to room'. As the names are the same, I take it that the 'lean-to room' leans on to George's house. A seamstress was less skilled than a dressmaker, who made a whole outfit for their customer.

Agricultural men of this time were still wearing collarless shirts with detachable collars, favouring a cloth tied loosely around the neck instead. A collar was only worn on Sundays, when it was attached to the shirt by means of a series of buttons.

## A Famous Visitor

**Mary Barker** (65) is a widow who works as a nurse. Her household consists of herself, her daughter Eliza (25) a domestic servant, her son John (23) a soldier, and **Henry Bass** (23), a visiting cricketer. Henry played for Kent and was just starting his first class career, after which he worked as a groundsman at Canterbury for 25 years. He is presumably visiting John.

## A Builder

**Alfred Foreman** (45) is still a builder, now employing 10 men and two boys. He lives with his wife Jane (40), his son Frank (16),who is still at school, **Emma Smith**, a servant, (21) **George Rogers** (24) a servant, lab, **James Tiggen** (19) an apprentice bricklayer and **John Hammond** (18) an apprentice carpenter. **William Pardoe** (31) a graduate in the university of Cambridge, is a visitor for the night.

He also rents land in the area, as shown by and advert is The South Eastern Gazette of 12th December 1871, when the field called Upper Lenty is offered for sale. It is noted that Mr Alfred Foreman is 'in occupation' as an annual tenant. There are fields on the 1839 tithe map of the area called Lenty and New Lenty, and also Upper and Lower fields. The field in question will be in this area, behind the new Kingfisher Place development.

Alfred's house is on a piece of land called Upper Lenty, on Shalmsford Street as a yearly tenant. This is described as a most desirable piece of building land with a frontage of 270 feet in Shalmsford Street. The name 'Lenty' appears on the 1842 tithe schedule as being in owned by Thomas Gambrill, but I cannot find whether or not it is still in his family in 1871.

Alfred is somewhat of a forward-thinker and it is reported In August 1872 that he puts on an annual entertainment for the men in his employ.

Parish Road was created at the expense of the South Eastern Railway when their railway crossed the existing road from Bolts Hill to Deanery Farm and Court Lodge. The level crossing now sits on the place where the old road originally ran. The road then turned east and ran across Deanery Meadow.

## In Parish Road are:

### The Village Bobby

**George Ross** (25) from Fifeshire is a police constable and has come to live here with his wife Eliza-ann (23) and their children Eliza (1) and James (2 months). By the time of the next census, the family have moved to Alkham and Eliza-Ann is looking after their seven children.

### Bolts Hill Farm

Also listed in Parish Road is **William Mouse** (56) who is a farmer employing 3 men and 4 boys on 100 acres of land. He lives with wife Mary (56) and son Samuel (17) who is listed as an employee on a farm. Also in the house is **Mary Fisher** (18) who works for them as a servant. I assume this is Bolts Hill Farm.

### An Engine Driver

**Thomas Cook** is an Engine Driver and Stoker (46), who will be working on the new railway. He lives with wife Ann (50) and three children. Mary (18) is a paper glazier at the paper mill in Chartham and her brother George (16) also works there as a paper maker. Frederick (8) goes to school, but will no doubt follow his siblings into the paper mill as it is the largest employer in the village.

Mary's job involves rubbing the newly-pressed sheets of paper with large flat stones to compress the surface and give it a sheen, which is back-breaking work as she leans over the table hour after hour. George's job title is more general and he was been involved in many of the operations at the factory.

By the time of the next census, the family have moved into Mill Cottages, Chartham, near the paper mill.

And in the Bolts Hill area of the village are:

## A Blacksmith

**Andrew H. Johnson** (52) is a blacksmith who lives with his wife Mary Ann (nee Aitken) (47). This family move about more than most families. In 1861 they were living in Dover, and by the time of the 1881 census they are living in Deal.

As well as acting as the village farrier, Andrew made all manner of metal objects, from saucepans to spits, and hinges to handtools.

## A Publican

'The Cross Key' pub is run by **Thomas Newington** (79), the publican. He lives with his wife, Ann (66), and his daughter Amelia Rudduck (46), Amelia's husband Isaac Rudduck (40), a dealer, and their daughters Elizabeth, (9) and Amy (4). Thomas's nephew **John Stevens** (19) (AL) is also living with them.

Interestingly, the census return doesn't specify what it is that Isaac deals in. It does note that he comes from Somersetshire, which makes it easier to trace his whereabouts in other returns. Some investigation shows us that he is later recorded as a Horse Trainer, so one would assume that it in horses that he deals.

A trawl of the newspaper archives reveals that Thomas was taken before the magistrate in 1867 for gambling. I assume that by 1871 this practice has now stopped.

Kentish Gazette 08 January 1867.

*ST. AUGUSTINE'S PETTY SESSIONS. SATURDAY, JANUARY, 5.*

*GAMBLING IN PUBLIC HOUSES.*

*Thomas Newington, of the 'Cross Keys Inn', Chartham, Victualler, was charged with having on the 22nd December, at the parish of Chartham, unlawfully and knowingly suffered gambling by divers persons, with a certain instrument called a Spinner or Rorolette, in his house there, for the purpose of winning certain pigs. Defendant pleaded "guilty," and after being cautioned by the Magistrates, he was fined 1 shilling and 10 shilllings costs.*

## Agricultural Labourers

The other people living in Shalmsford those living in families where the head of the household is an agricultural or general labourer. The Employment Act of 1870 raised the minimum working age to 10, but many children would still have been working before this age, as their income could mean the survival or otherwise of weaker family members. The working week had been cut to around 55 hours a week in the towns, although rural workers would still often work dawn till dusk, especially when work such as haymaking and getting in the wheat or hop harvest were time sensitive.

## Shalmsford Street

### Small, But Perfectly Formed

**Edward Pay** (57) (AL) lives with wife Eliza (47) and Mary Ann (12). This family stay in the village, and we later see Mary Ann marry and take a house here, too.

### Always Pregnant

**Jesse Hoare** (28) (AL) lives with his wife Louisa (nee Reynolds) (30) and their children Harry (7), Emily (5), Annie (3), George (5 months). Two more children follow before Louisa's death, but the story does have a happy ending as we see in successive records. One important chore of the pregnant mother was the need to sew baby clothes for the new arrival. Luckily, Louisa had a stock of these saved from the births of her other children.

### Enjoying Grandma's Cooking

**Richard Hoare** (AL) (47) and Elizabeth (59) still have **William Cook**, their grandson, living with them. At thirteen, William is already working as an agricultural labourer. Richard's sons and daughters have all now left home, but William has stayed with his grandparents.

### A Young Family

Next, **Henry Cork** (AL) (24) and Esther (nee Hayward) (25) who have two children, George (2), Jane (11 months). This family welcomes more children, and it is lovely to see them grow and make homes for themselves in the area. Baby James joins the family in May 1872, but he dies the same year, but their next child, Frederick arrives in 1874 and survives to adulthood.

There is another child, Alfred, born in Mary 1878, but I cannot find what happens to him. He does not appear on the 1881 census.

### A Baby Sister for the Boys

**Edward Mumford** (33) (AL) lives with Phoebe (nee Hoare) (30), and their children Richard (9), William Jesse (6), Lucy (2 months). Lucy was baptized on April 2nd; the same day the census was taken. Phoebe is Jesse Hoare's sister, daughter to Richard and Elizabeth.

The world looks bright for this family at the moment. However, towards the end of the century, Edward falls into depression and tries to take his own life.

## Bavins for Firewood

**Richard Baldock** (29) is a bavin maker. He and his wife Emma Elizabeth (25) have three daughters: Eliza (6), Kate (5) and Annie Maria (1). These three children are joined by three more by the time the 1881 census is taken. Also in the house is **Robert Lipperwell** (AL) (22) an unmarried man, who is their boarder.

A bavin is a bunch of small twigs used as firewood. A man could make up to 100 in a day, while a child would make half that many. They were paid piece-work, so any extra money the children made as they got older would help to feed the family. Even those children who were not formally employed played a part, ensuring that the best possible piece-rate was achieved.

A bavin-maker would wear long leather gloves to protect his arms as he put them around the bundle of twigs before tying them. The twigs were the by-product of coppicing or felling timber and the resulting faggot was about 3ft long and 24in round.

The couple's fourth daughter is born at the end of the summer. Rosa Matilda is baptized on September 3rd.

Their next child, born in April 1873, dies later the same year aged 3 months.

## A Fight in the Night

The children of **William Hall**, (43) (AL) and Elizabeth (41) range from 3 to 18, and those who currently live at home are Amelia (13), William (11) (AL), Ann (7), Thomas (5), Eliza (3).

A quick look at The Whitstable Times and Herne Bay Herald dated 19th December 1874 reveals a court case heard by the Canterbury County Court about an altercation between William Hall and Thomas Baldock, his next door neighbour. Given that this was three years after the census, it is likely that Thomas was a relative of Richard Baldock who has moved to the area.

After leaving 'The Cross Keys' at 11pm on Saturday 19th September, the men argued and Thomas Baldock punched William Hall on the jaw. William had had his hands in his pockets at the time of the blow and he fell heavily, hitting his head, which knocked him senseless. Mr Cook, another neighbour, had helped him indoors where he wife washed and dressed the wound. On Monday, the surgeon visited Mr Hall and reported to the court that he had found him insensible and suffering from paralysis of his left arm and leg.

William said at the trial that he was earning 35s or £2 a week before the accident, but had only been able to work two or three days a week since the accident and that only recently.

Thomas Baldock's attourney said that William had in fact only tripped over a bundle of hop bines in the dark, while his wife was pushing him into the house. Emma Baldock, Thomas' wife, Sophia Howshaw, PC Ford and Richard Pay, who were also neighbours, were called as witnesses, although Sophia and PC Ford were found to be too tipsy to be credible. However, after noting that both parties were somewhat culpable, the court found for the plaintiff, and ordered Thomas to pay £10 in costs in instalments of 10s a month.

This case gives us a detailed insight into the lives of the people I have been recording. We now know how much they earnt, and how late they stayed out at the pub on a Saturday night. We know that the women relied on the money they earn from helping with the hop harvest, and that some people were tipsy when they turned up at court! We also have a little glimpse of which families live near to each other.

Despite this altercation, William stays in the area for another twenty years.

## A New Husband for Mary

**James Stacey** (32) a labourer and Mary (41) have three children at home. Jane (14), Mary (7), James (5). They have an extra income in the money they get from **Elizabeth Lorum** a factory girl who boards with them must be a relative of Mary, as Lorum was her maiden name. You will remember that Mary was previously married to Obediah Solomon, who is Jane's father, before she married James. As Jane was only two when her mother remarried, she has taken her step-father's name.

## A Canadian in the Making

**Henry Cork** (40) a bricklayers labourer and his wife Jane (44) live with five of their children: George (18) (AL), Sarah (10) Edward (7), John (4), Charles (2). Daughters Charlotte, Emily and Eliza have all left home, but there is one more child to add. Jesse is born in the autumn and baptized on November 5th 1871.

Henry's son George goes on to marry Jane Beaney, with whom he has nine children. He has moved away from Shalmsford Street by the time of the next census and in his fifties he takes the extraordinary step of emigrating to Canada, and lives in Ontario until his death in 1927.

## Representing Ireland

**George Sims** (39) (AL) and Ann (31), have one son, John (10), and three daughters: Sarah (8), Alice (5) and Harriott (2). George has only the one son to keep him company in a family of women and goes on to have four more daughters. Ann is from Longford in Ireland.

The next baby, another girl, is born in the

summer, and is baptized Mary Elizabeth on September 3rd 1871.

## A Single Father

**Robert Pay** (39) is a labourer and seems to be widowed. He lives with his daughter Emily (17) who is a servant out of place, by which I take to mean she is 'between jobs'. Eliza is 14, and at 13 William works as a factory boy. The other two people in the house are **Caroline Hook** (27) an unmarried woman who is as their housekeeper, and her daughter Kate Hook (6). There is a burial record for Caroline Hook, aged 7, dated December 13th 1871, which I assume is this child.

## Births and Deaths

**John Harlow** (30) (AL), has a wife, Charlotte (nee Marsh) (28) and four children: Rachael (10), William James (7), Mary (4) and Thomas (1). The church records show that the couple had a daughter called Sarah Ann in the summer of 1867 with a family address of Box Trees. She only lived for 8 days, so does not appear on this census. This may be the reason the family moved to Shalmsford Street.

I have also found a burial record for Alfred Harlow, who died aged 8 months in March 1873. I cannot find a birth or baptism record for this child, so I cannot be sure he was in this family. There is also a burial record for Emma Harlow in May 1873, who was just 2 days old when she died. Again, I cannot be sure she is from this family.

## Working with Wood

**George Neame** (35) is a woodman and wattle weaver. His wife Mary (29) must have her hands full with Nehemiah (7), Sarah (5) Eunice (2) Jacob (5 months), who are not yet old enough to help her with the major housework, but are old enough to keep her on her toes.

A wattle was a moveable length of woven fence that was mainly used in sheep farming, about three foot tall, called a hurdle in other parts of the country. The wood is cut and dried, then woven around nine uprights, twisting it at the end to break the fibres: wattle weavers had very strong wrists.

## A Paper-mill Worker

**William Ansley** (62) (AL) and Sarah (62) have one daughter still at home. Sophy (22) is not yet married and works as a paper sorter. Over the next ten years, Sophy does marry and lives in the village with her new family.

## A Young Family

**George Lyons** (27) (AL) and Sarah Ann (nee Epps) (23) were married in 1869. They have two daughters: Ellen Epps (2), Sarah Ann Lyons (1). Ellen Epps is Sarah's first child, born out of wedlock or to a previous husband, and she soon changes her name to Ellen Lyons. George and

Sarah have four more children over the next ten years.

## Another Spinster Daughter

**James Austen** (61) (AL) and Elizabeth (58) live with their unmarried daughter, Elizabeth (26). There is some documentary evidence of Elizabeth marrying William Ward, but the date given is 1869. It could be that Elizabeth is already married, but that James was so used to giving his daughter's maiden name that he just made a mistake.

James Austen dies later this year, aged 62. He was buried on July 7th 1871.

## Waiting for Marriage

**William Friar** (AL) (58) and Sarah (59) live with their daughter Jane (24) who is also unmarried. Jane has returned to live with her parents, but their other daughter, Eliza, has now left. In a few years, Jane marries Thomas Ballard and stays nearby.

## The Quiet Before the Storm

**James Smith** (30) a labourer is married to Sarah (21). They move out of Shalmsford and into Mill Row, near the paper mill and by the time of the next census have eight children.

## Another Branch of the Spillett Family

**George Spillett** (37) (AL) has four children at home with him and his wife Harriett (40): Edward (13) (AL), William (6), Mary (4), Edith (1). These people are surrounded by aunts and uncles and stay in the village for years. The family is extended by one when Edgar is born. He is baptized on November 5th 1871.

## Court Lodge Cottages

**William Spillett** (43) (AL) and his wife Mary Ann (nee Richardson) (35) live in a cottage at Court Lodge. They have three children at home: Charlotte (17), Elizabeth (14) and Jeanette (7). They have two boarders, which filled the house, but in the long run, made life more comfortable for the family. The boarders were **Edward Fryer** (21) and **George Hoare** (17) who both worked as agricultural labourers.

After this census, we do not see this family again, and I assume that William moves to another village in search of work. He might even take them into Canterbury, as it is about this time that the rural economy starts to give way to the larger urban economies.

Also at Court Lodge are **John Harvey** (57) (AL) with his wife Susannah (58). This family, too, move out before the next census.

## Trying for a Baby

**Henry Spillett** (40), William's brother, is also a labourer and is married to Sophie (37) a village school mistress in the infants school. The couple have no children at this point, but they do later adopt a little girl.

## A Broken-hearted Widower

The next household also sees a widowed man who has given room to a lady who can act as housekeeper and mother to the children. **Harry Spillett** (52) (AL) is Nephew to Willam and Henry and has been left with four children: Edwin (11), Phoebe (8), James (6) and Alfred (3) now his wife Phoebe has died. Widower **Susanne Godden** (62) is the housekeeper. Since Harry's wife Phoebe passed away in 1870, his three oldest sons have moved out.

I do not know the exact chain of events, but I do know that Harry never remarries. I also know that by 1891, Susanne is in the workhouse in Bridge.

## At the End of Their Days

**William Cozens** (60) (AL) is married to Ann (55) and was recorded as being a gardener on the previous census. William dies in 1874, and even though I cannot find a death date for Ann, this is the last time we see her in Shalmsford.

## He Couldn't Live Without Her

**Thomas Homersham** (85) formerly a labourer, lives with his wife Charlotte (75). This is the last we see of this couple, as Thomas and Charlotte both die in 1877. Charlotte passed away in August, and Thomas followed her in December of the same year.

## Still Living with Mum

**Edward Link** (28) (AL) lives with Jane (48), who is listed as his wife, but who I think must be his mother.

## An Apprentice Blacksmith

John Link (39) is a widower and works as an agricultural labourer, but his son James (15) has found a place as an apprentice blacksmith. His son Edward (11) (AL) is already out at work with his father. The house is looked after by **Elizabeth Reynolds** (60), widow who is their housekeeper.

## The Boys Have Left Home

**George Cork** (54) (AL) is married to Elizabeth (59). Henry has now left home and has his own house in Chartham. Their son William has moved into Rattington Street, where he is working as a servant, and he stays here when he marries and starts his own family.

## Three Generations in One House

**Sarah Spickett**, widow, (65) formerly the wife of an agricultural labourer lives with Sarah (28) her unmarried daughter who works as a paper sorter, Walter, (5) her grandson and **John Marsh** (53) her widowed brother. This little family group have mainly stayed together, although Ann has left, and now it is time for Sarah to go, as she dies next year.

## A Budding Romance

**Esther Vincer** (53) is still unmarried and gives her occupation as 'formerly labourer's daughter'. Her daughter Eliza (23) is a rag cutter at the paper mill. Eliza's daughter Mary (2) also lives here along with **Henry Wright** (23) their boarder, who is a labourer. I wonder if Esther has spotted the romance developing between Eliza and Henry who marry before the next census.

The rags used in the paper-making industry had to be cut up before they were sorted, cleaned, washed in caustic soda and processed into pulp. The women cut the rags using razor-sharp knives to cut the rags into small pieces.

## A New Life Down Under

**Sarah Washford** (78) was formerly a labourer's wife, but is now a widow. She lives with her grandson, **James Goodale** (16) (AL) at the moment, but she dies in 1873. James marries Angelina Finn in 1873 and they emigrate to Australia.

## Two Households in One

**Charlotte Wraight** (68), now a widow, was also formerly a labourer's wife. She lives with her granddaughter Elizabeth (12), along with her son Thomas (29) and his wife Mary Ann (24). **John Daniels** (24) (AL) is a boarder in their home. Charlotte's daughter Sarah has left home, taking her own daughter with her. I wonder how happy the mixing of the two households is, as Charlotte moves into Cantebury by the time of the next census to live with her daughter Harriett Martin.

## A Father Nicknamed Thoggin

**William Gipson** (48) is still a labourer. His large household consists of his wife, Sarah (44), and his older children who work in the paper mill: Frances (18), Rosa (16) and Jesse (14), and his younger two children Lilley (12) and John (10). **Roger "Thoggin" Hill** is Sarah's widowed father (83) and was formerly an agricultural labourer who was born in Devon, like his daughter.

The name of young John is recorded in the School Ledger after having attended for less than a week, when he was flogged for 'defying his teacher and creating an uproar in the school'. I can only imagine how this uproar was created, but it is also recorded that he made use of some very bad language before accepting his punishment.

Their boarder Henry Cook has now moved out. William and Sarah are lucky that they have been able to keep all their family with them for such a long time.

The family grows in 1873 when Rosa gives birth to Mabel. Even after her marriage to George Bains in 1875, she and Mabel continue to live with her parents for a while. By 1891, however, they have a home in Rattington Street.

The family move to Bridge, where they can be found on the 1871 census, but they are back in Shalmsford in 1881 under the name Gibson. The two names seem to be relatively easily interchanged on both civil and parish records, which could be in part to the Kentish accent.

## This Family Enjoys Five Wages

**James Link** (65) (AL), Jane (61), live with their unmarried sons Henry (25) (AL) and William (19) (AL). Their daughter Jane (19), William's twin, is a glazier at the paper mill. The couple's grandson James (4) also lives in the house and is presumable Jane's son. Jane marries Thomas Cavill Newton later this same year

## The Sister-in-Law Moves In

**Thomas Bartlett** (40) (AL), lives with his wife Ann (50) and her sister **Jane Davis** (25).

## Was Thomas Happy?

**Thomas Cork** (56) (AL) and Mary Ann (58) share their home with members of Mary Ann's family: **John Austen** (33) (AL), born in Devon and George Austen (29) (AL) are Mary's sons from before her marriage, and Judith Austen (62), a village school mistress working with the infants, and Thomas Austen (60) (AL), are her siblings. Also in the house is **Charlotte Eldridge** (7) who was born in London and is still at school. Charlotte may be linked to the Austen family, or may have been taken in as a foster child. She is listed as a boarder, as are the Austen family.

As a point of interest, Thomas Cork's brother George, and his wife Elizabeth also live in Shalmsford Street.

Mary dies in 1876 and Thomas moves in with his brother George.

## Twenty Happy Years in the Village

**Lydia Sakree** (74) was widowed before she moved to Shalmsford Street and she dies in 1874, so this is the last we see of her. When she died, she left £50, which went to Thomas Williams, a blacksmith from Waltham, and the son of her legatee. This leads me to the conclusion that she had written a will in which her married daughter was to inherit, but the daughter had passed away before Lydia did.

## A Second Woodreeve

Next are **George Hoare**, (69) a woodreeve who lives with his wife Mary (67), and **Thomas Neame** (72) a widowed labourer who boards with them. George and Mary did previously supplement their income by taking in a boarder, but

Thomas is a new addition to the household. He is the father-in-law of George's daughter Mary Ann, who married George Neame, Thomas' son in 1863. Their children have now left home, but many still live in Shalmsford. The job of woodreeve was somewhat similar to a forest ranger, as he would have been responsibility for a stretch of woodland.

The fact that there are two woodreeves in Shalmsford Street alone shows the reliance of the population on the surrounding countryside. Wood was needed for houses, furniture, carts, tools and for fuel as well as for use in gates and fence-making. Coppiced wood was also essential in the husbandry of hop fields.

## Still Happily Unmarried

**John Young** (51) is still unmarried and is listed as a former carter. It is noted that his sight is now defective, which explains why he has stopped working. The census does not tell us how he earns a living.

## Deanery Cottages

At Deanery Cottage, **James Dixon** (65) (AL) and wife Elizabeth (64) live with daughter Mercy (24) who is still unmarried. Mercy dies in 1872 and her father follows her soon afterwards.

## Parish Road

Parish Road is now an extension of Bolts Hill, taking the traveller into the heart of Chartham Village. This 'new' road was created at the expense of SER when the railway line crossed the existing road that turned left by the school and passed by The Deanery and across Deanery Meadow into the village. It has not been seen on the census before as it was not flanked by any residential dwellings.

## A New Baby For Edward

Next in the register are **Edward Hoare** (24) (AL) and Hariette (nee Vidgeon) (23) with baby Harriette (8 months). Baby Harriette was the first of many children; by the time of the 1881 census they had four more.

## Widow and Widower find Happiness Together

**William Dale** (45) (AL) and wife Susan (43) live with William's children Elizabeth Ann (19) who is an employee at the paper factory, George (12) and Ros-anna (9) and Susan's children from her previous marriage: Edgar Lunnun (11) and Jane Lunnuns (5). William and Susan married in 1870 after the death of their spouses. We can watch this family as they stay in the area and the children grow up, marry and have children of their own.

## A Third Woodreeve

**Thomas E. Dixon**, woodreeve and gatemaker, (36) lives with his wife Elizabeth (35) and their five children Edwin (8), Thomas (6), Charles (5), Mary Ann (3) and Ellen (2). The family move away after this census.

## An Annual Contract

**George Featherstone** (51) is a farm servant. Recorded in the house are his wife Jane (52), his sons Thomas (15) (AL) and William (10), daughters Ann (8), and Elizabeth (20). On the last census, this family were living in Horton Chapel Lane.

George's occupation is less secure than farm labourers, who were employed on a more-or-less permanent basis. Farm servants were engaged at the annual hiring fair for one year only. However, Thomas was bringing in an income and William and Ann were earning money from casual labour.

## A Houseful of Men

**William Fisher** (59) works as a carman labourer. A carman was similar to a carter i.e. someone who transported goods. Whether or not this was horsedrawn or on the railway, I do not know. He and his wife Ann (nee Link) (42) were married in 1855 and they live with their sons James (15) (AL), John (13) who is employed in paper manufactory, along with Charles (10) and Edward (3 months). This family continue to live in the area for many years.

William and Ann still have one more child to welcome to their family. Clara Jane is baptized in Chartham church on October 1st 1871. She does not stay with them long, and is buried on November 20th 1872 aged 14 months.

## Boxtrees House

Boxtrees House is home to **Amy Philpott** (59) formerly a labourers wife, Lydia (31), a paper sorter, Eliza (24) a dressmaker, James (14) (AL), George, Amy's grandson (5) who is still at school along with **Eliza Friar** (45) who boards with them. She is married and works as a paper sorter. Lydia goes on to marry Edward Link by the time of the 1881 census. George is Lydia's son.

## Bolts Hill

The next four households are particularly interesting. A notice in the South Eastern Gazette dated 12th December 1871 advertises for sale seven lots of land on Bolts Hill. The first lot is a 'respectable dwelling house, three cottages, barn, stabling, cowhouse, piggeries, lodge, yards and gardens with three pieces of very fertile arable land, called Bolt's Hill Field, Half Craft and Elm Field'. It further states that the occupants are Mr James Hearn (who does not appear on the census returns for this area), George Cook, Henry Hoare, William Gibbs and Thomas Streeting. James Hearn is noted as being the holder of a 14-year lease for the properties as from 1864, but that they are being sold by the mortgagee. Who, out of these four people listed below, live in the house and which families had the cottages is not shown. My guess is that it was George Cook.

**George Cook** (38) works at the paper mill as a paper bleacher. His wife is Harriotte

(37) and the children are Richard (8), Frances (5) and Thomas (2). George's father, Stephen Cook, is now a widower (75) and lives with them. He was formerly a sawyer by trade.

**Henry Hoare** (26) (AL) is married to Maryann (nee Eastland) (24). They have two children: Caroline (3) and Emily (1).

**William Gibbs** (AL) (49) shares his home with his wife Mary Ann (48).

**Thomas Streeting** (34) House decorator, plumber etc, lives with his wife Eliza (34) and their children Thomas (10) Arthur (5) and Walter (3).

The next lot advertised for auction is a respectable brick-dwelling house with nearly three-quarters of an acre of garden ground adjacent to Lot 1, occupied by Mr Henry Hearn. His details appear on the census as below:

**Henry J. Hearn** (37). He gives his occupation as Farmers Son in Charge and is son to James Hearn, who lives in Harbledown, but owns land in Chartham and Shalmsford. Henry lives with his family, wife Eliza (37) and children Harry (8) Ambrose (6) Sydney (4) and William (2). Previously, he was living in a bachelor pad with Ambrose Hukins, but he has now married Eliza Willcocks.

All these properties were on the northeast side of Bolts Hill, still clearly within the confines of the Shalmsford Street hamlet.

Elm Field was listed on the 1842 Tithe Map and was shown as belonging to John Collard Sankey and in the occupation of William Handcock. It is a large field, occupying the whole of the south side of Bobbin Lodge Hill (previously Pay's Lane)Other Records

As with the other decades, there are people who appear on the church records and in other documentary evidence that are not recorded on the national census. The following information is taken from the parish records of St Marys, Chartham, and so record deaths and those births registered with the church. There was no legal requirement to register a birth with the Church of England, and many more may have been registered with either the Wesleyan or Primitive Methodist church.

- Roger Hill lived in Shalmsford Street and died in April 1871 aged 85.

- Thomas and Sophia Howshaw, who are mentioned in the altercation between Messrs Hall and Baldock do not appear on the census. However, there is a record of a Harry Howshaw aged 12 who dies in 1872. I wonder if this family had recently moved into the area. There is also a burial record for James Howshaw dated 27th October. He died when he was 57. I wonder if this is the same family.

- There is a burial record for James William Cork, aged 66, entered on 25th July 1872.

- Henry Link of Shalmsford Street dies in June 1879 aged 33.

- John and Hannah Goodale lived in Shalmsford Street, and John was a plumber and glazier. Their baby Mary Ada was born in 1870.

- John and Charlotte Harlow, noted last census for being absent from the records, appear in the parish records at the birth of their son Thomas Edward.

- Clara Maria Tyler is born to George and Eliza who also lived in Shalmsford Street.

- William Alfred Cork was born to George and Harriet of Bolts Hill in 1871.

- Elizabeth Lyons, daughter of George and Sarah Ann was born in March 1872, but died aged 3 months.

- Florence Jane was born in 1872 to James and Sarah Smith

- John and Charlotte Harlow welcomed George in April 1872.

- John and Harriet Gibson had Jesse with them for only 14 days. He was baptized in April 1872 but died two weeks later

- Richard Jones and his wife Emily had a baby called Annie and when she was baptized in September 1872, they had their other daughter Jane, who had been born in March 1868 baptized at the same time.

- Harry and Frances Baldock's son Henry was born in 1878.

- Rose Fox was baptised while she was living with her parents in Shalmsford Street in 1878, but they moved into Chartham before the 1881 census.

- Henry and Mary Hoare, welcomed baby Phoebe in 1872.

Shalmsford Street, looking south from Ransley's Farm, left

# The 1880s

The 1880s was a snowy decade, following the wetness of the 1870s. 1880 started the trend with snow in October, and 1881 was the year of the Great Storm, when almost all the roads in Kent were so frozen they were impassable. Almost every winter of the decade then had snow, while the summers were particularly dry.

During the blizzards in January, which brought with it a hurricane-force wind, wreaking havoc on the Kent coast the promenade at Folkestone was washed away, and a train at Ramsgate was buried under 16 feet of snow. Post Office telegraphs were suspended, as were the mail trains, and at Woolwich 26 barges were lost.

The impact on the labouring classes of Shalmsford can be imagined, with families forced to stay indoors, huddled together for warmth around fires loaded with whatever combustible materials they could find, wearing every item of clothing they owned. Outdoor work was been suspended during this time, with workers left out-of-pocket at the end of each week.

Later in the decade, the country was struck by drought, and Kent suffered badly, with the harvest being severely damaged.

A more pleasant fact is that this is the decade in which the world accepted Greenwich Mean Time as the official time zone. Also, local people would have been amazed to see the aurora borealis in November 1882. The local newspaper reports that on the night of November 17th red and green clouds of colour were seen in the sky.

Urban workers were given the vote in 1867, and in 1884, rural workers were afforded the same privilege. I wonder how many men in the village took up the offer.

The first meeting of Kent County Council took place in 1889, consisting of a group of 72 elected councillors, who met in Maidstone. Opinions were divided on whether this was a good thing.

A rise in the number of children registered regularly in the school log books is now seen, as the Education Act of 1880 saw the enforcement of the requirement that every child should attend school from the age of five for a minimum of five years. This was brought in with the previous Education Act, but was never properly regulated. School fees were raised in 1883, and were charged on a sliding scale, according to a rudimentary means test performed by the School Board. Fees ranged from 1d per week for a labourers second child to 6d for the children of tradesmen and farmers.

The village of Shalmsford joined in the celebrations of Queen Victoria's Golden Jubilee in June 1887, when there was a fete on Chartham village green, with tea provided for the aged, the poor and for children, along with sports and a chance to listen to The City Band. Everyone was granted a day's holiday and the day ended with fireworks.

The Kentish Gazette also reports that a separate celebration was held 'At Shalmsford', clearly showing that the village was still regarded as a separate hamlet. Alfred Foreman gave a garden party for young people aged 14-25, providing a sit-down tea for 55 people. They were joined later in the evening by 27 tenants who gave a rousing rendition of The National Anthem to accompany a firework display and then danced on the lawn until gone 11 o'clock. The total number of people attending was estimated to be around 200.

Villagers would also have been able to see some of the Golden Jubilee Beacons which straddled the country.

# 1881 Census

This census recorded the population's whereabouts on the night of 3rd April 1881 and the enumerator was George Homersham. This is the same George Homersham that appeared on the 1871 census living with his parents. He is now shown living with his wife and has taken over running the family's grocer's business. The census returns form lists all the people staying at the given address that night.

The enumeration district is shown as 'Part of the Parish of Chartham, including Perry Farm, Thruxted Farm, Underdown Cottages, Mystole House and Cottages, Long Neck, Pickleden, Boltshill, Chartham Deanery, Court Lodge Farm, Rattington Street, Horton Chapel Farm and Cottages, and the Cottages around the Asylum.' Someone has added in a different hand 'and Shalmsford Street'.

Occupations in Shalmsford, 1881

| | | |
|---|---|---|
| Agricultural labourer | 63 | 33% |
| Worker at the paper mill | 15 | 8% |
| Domestic servant/charwoman | 12 | 6% |
| Carrier/carter | 8 | 4% |
| Bricklayer's labourer | 7 | 4% |
| Bricklayer | 6 | 3% |
| Carpenter | 6 | 3% |
| Platelayer | 5 | 3% |
| Gardener | 4 | 2% |
| Shoemaker | 4 | 2% |
| Teacher | 4 | 2% |
| Farmer | 3 | 2% |
| Grocer | 3 | 2% |
| Housekeeper | 3 | 2% |
| Labourer | 3 | 2% |
| Laundress | 3 | 2% |
| Licenced victualler | 3 | 2% |
| Apprentice | 2 | 1% |
| Builder | 2 | 1% |
| Licenced hawker | 2 | 1% |
| Nurse | 2 | 1% |
| P.C. | 2 | 1% |
| Paper maker | 2 | 1% |
| Baker | 1 | <1% |
| Barmaid | 1 | <1% |

| Blacksmith | 1 | <1% |
|---|---|---|
| Butcher | 1 | <1% |
| Coal merchant | 1 | <1% |
| Confectioner | 1 | <1% |
| Engine driver | 1 | <1% |
| Farm bailiff | 1 | <1% |
| Gamekeeper | 1 | <1% |
| Groom | 1 | <1% |
| Horse dealer | 1 | <1% |
| Insurance agent | 1 | <1% |
| Mariner | 1 | <1% |
| Milkman | 1 | <1% |
| Needlewoman | 1 | <1% |
| Plumber | 1 | <1% |
| Porter | 1 | <1% |
| River watcher | 1 | <1% |
| Shop worker | 1 | <1% |
| Telegraphist | 1 | <1% |
| Wheelwright | 1 | <1% |
| Wood dealer | 1 | <1% |
| Worker at the asylum | 1 | <1% |
| | 191 | |

This is the first census when people with identifiable trades and professions outnumber those who are general agricultural workers. Many more people in Shalmsford are employed in the paper mill and now work is becoming available at the St Augustine's Lunatic Asylum.

There are more people than ever living in the village, with 96 households recorded on this census. The demographic has now changed considerably. Whereas in the last decade, there was an increased number of older people, that number has now shrunk again to 20 and the number of children under 10 has doubled to 139.

# Agricultural Labourers

Those still recorded as agricultural labourers are now in the minority. We see the same faces in the village, as families expand and children grow to adulthood. The works has changed slightly, and so has the clothing. The old fashion of wearing off-white undyed cotton, heavy but hard-wearing has now been discarded in favour of the darker clothing, previously only worn by city-dwellers. Woollen jackets, similar to donkey jackets, were worn to keep out the weather, and with their dense, felted fabric they provided an effective defence against the elements.

These are families where the head of the household has identified himself as an agricultural labourer (AL). Again, many of the older children are working, some in recognised trades of higher social status than their parents.

## On Bolts Hill

## Only Edward is still at School

The first household is that of **William Hall** (45) (AL) with his wife Elizabeth (53) and their sons Thomas (16) and Edward (8). Both William and Thomas work as agricultural labourers and Edward is at school. The family previously lived in Shalmsford Street and continue to live in the village in 1891.

## Five Children for Sarah

**George Lyons** (35) (AL) is still married to Sarah (nee Epps) (32) and they now have five children at home, Sarah (11), Albert (8), Mary (6), Emily (4) and Frederick (1). The family is not yet complete, as they have four more children by the time of the 1891 census. Ellen, their eldest has left home, possibly to take up a post as a servant locally. Sarah, Albert and Mary are listed as scholars.

## Seven for Mary

**George Moat** is listed next on the census, as they are in 1891, so it is possible they live next door. George (33) and Mary (32) have seven children at home, Lewis (12), Matilda (10), James (8), John (5), Mary (4), Emma (3) and Horace (1). The 1891 census shows us that, like the Lyons family, they go on to have several more. Lewis and George work as agricultural labourers, but all the other children, excepting the two youngest, go to school.

## Court Lodge Cottages

In the cottages at Court Lodge are **William Dale** (56) (AL) and his family. All the children shown on the 1871 census have now moved away from home. William lives with his wife Susan (52) and his son-in-law **John Simmons** (25). John has married one of William and Susan's daughter. Also in the house are Stephen (9) and Bertha (6). The couple also have three boarders, **Thomas Keeler** (26), **James Spickett** (20) and **Louis Vaughan** (16) who all works as agricultural labourers. As boarders, they would eat with the family as well as sleep in the house.

**William Kenton** (65) (AL) and his wife Fanny (54) are also newcomers and live at Court Lodge cottages.

## Box Tree Cottages

**James Lawton** (58) (AL) from Hinxhill in Kent with his wife Ann (50) live in Box Tree cottages.

Also in Box Trees cottages, we come to another family we recognise. **Henry Wright** (45) (AL) has married Eliza Vincer (36) and her daughter Mary (12) has also taken her stepfather's name. Their own children are Eliza (8), Caroline (5) and Henry (3). Eliza's mother Esther Vincer (58) is listed as a pauper and lives with them. She no doubt loves to help with the children, but the three eldest are now at school.

## Coming up Roses

**Joseph Ladd** (69) (AL) was born in Chartham, but is new to Shalmsford. He lives with his wife Susannah (65) and their son Charles (36), a labourer in Box

Tree Cottages. Having previously lived in Radigund Street, they have recently returned from Goudhurst where he had a job as a gardener.

## In Shalmsford Street

### A Familiar Face

**Charles Vincer** (48), who we have seen in the past two census returns is still in Shalmsford Street with his wife Eliza (47) and their son Charles, who is now 10. Charles Snr still works as an agricultural labourer and his son goes to school, although his daughter has left home.

### A Single Father

We met **George Spillett** (48) (AL) in the 1861 census when he was still in his twenties. His wife Harriet has died, and he now has five children at home; John, George, Edward and Mary, have left home and Willie (16) and Edith, (11) have been joined by Edgar (9) and Frederick (5). Willie works as a farm servant, while the three younger children go to school.

### An All-Male Household

George's brother, **Henry Spillett** (63) (AL) lives with his son Alfred (19) (AL). These two are relatively well-off with two wages and no dependents, but I wonder how close they are. If they live together for necessity only, and also work together, the atmosphere would be strained, to say the least.

### George is Surrounded by Women

We meet **George Sims** (48) (AL) again in the next house with his wife Ann (46) and their growing family of daughters. Their oldest daughter Alice (16) works as a glazier at the paper mill, while the three younger girls Mary (9) Ann (6) and Clara (4) go to school.

### A Late Marriage

We also met **Edward Link** (37) (AL) in the last census, living with his mother Ann, but he has now married Lydia (nee Philpott) (40). We previously saw Lydia living with her mother Amy and her brothers and sisters. Lydia's son George Philpott (15) lives with the family, and Edward and Lydia now have four children of their own, Lucy (7), Charles (5), James (3) and Sydney (1). At 15, George is old enough to work and earns a living as a general labourer.

### Two Wages Make Life Easier

**John Hulse** (46) also works as a general labourer and supports his family with the help of his son John (15) (AL). They have five people depending on them: John Snr's wife Charlotte (42), their daughters Jane (8) and Annie (5) and two younger sons, Harry (3) and George (1). The girls go to school, while the boys are still at home.

## A Move to the Country in their Later Years

**Charles Spillett** (65) (AL) lives with his wife Margaret (61) who is from Folkestone. There are many of the Spillett family in the area, but Charles is a newcomer.

## Age is not an Issue

**Samuel Harlow** (57) (AL) must have very little income, and yet has a large family. His wife Ann (nee Marsh)(34) is much younger than he and will have her hands full looking after their children. The oldest son, Frederick (14) brings in a wage as an agricultural labourer like his father, but the others are at school or at home. Samuel (11), Herbert (10) and Walter (6) are at school while Anna (3) and William (2) are at home.

## A Fledgling Family

Another small family comes next. **George Cole** (30) (AL) from Chilham lives with Amelia (32) from Boughton. Their children George (4) and Alice (1) are too young to be at school.

## Lucky Edward is Still at School

**William Fisher** (64) (AL) lives with his wife Ann (50) and three of their children. The older boy, Frederick (17) (AL) works, but Edward (13) is still at school. This was unheard-of when the Shalmsford Street census was first taken in 1841. The youngest child is Ann (7), is not listed as being at school. She may suffer from a chronic illness that prevents her from going, or perhaps the enumerator just forgot to add that little piece of information.

## A Late Marriage for Winifred

**John Barker** (34) (AL) was born in Chartham, but his wife Winifred (nee Greenstreet) (31) comes from Wye. They were married in 1877 and now have two children, Ann (2) and Edith (1).

## Registered Blind

**John Fearn** (57) (AL) lives with his wife Sarah (61). Tritton Adam's wife Rebecca is his sister. Sarah was born in Bearstead and is now registered as blind. She passes away in October 1881.

## A Happy Threesome

**George Hoare** (78)(AL) and his wife Mary (76) still have widower **Thomas Neame** (82) living with them as a boarder. The income from this is no doubt very welcome.

## Three Generations

**William Ansley** (72) (AL) and his wife have stayed in Shalmsford Street, although we see a few changes to the household. His wife Sarah (72) is still alive and their daughter Sophia (32) still lives with them, but they have been joined by Sophia's new husband **William Bartlett** (43) who is an engine driver at the paper mill. Sophia and William's first child has been named after her mother.

## This Family Stick Together

**Richard Hoare** (76) (AL), George's brother, and his wife Elizabeth (69) also have one lodger, **Charles Coltham** (20), a carpenter from Kingstone.

## Proud of her Sons

**Margaret Linkin** (nee Shilling) (60) is a widow and is the head of her household and is recorded as being an annuitant. An annuitant is usually someone in receipt of a pension. However, as her husband Robert was an agricultural labourer until his death, it is likely that she is living on the incomes of her sons and too proud to admit it. Her two sons Edward (24) and Isaac (22), the youngest of her nine children, both work as agricultural labourers, while her granddaughter **Louisa Burchett** (9) is still at school. I have failed to find the name of Louisa's mother, but it is most likely that it is Margaret and Robert's first child, Louisa.

## Jane's Mother Pays her Way

**Thomas Ballard** (31) (AL) is from Charing. He lives with his wife Jane (nee Friar) (33) who is from Chartham. They live with Jane's daughter from before the marriage, **Ada Friar** (6) who goes to school and Thomas' two daughters Eliza (2) and Florence (6 months). Also in the house is **Sarah Friar** (69) who is Jane's widowed mother. She works as a charwoman.

## Getting On

**Edward Pay** (67) (AL) lives with his wife Eliza (59).

## Two Johns

**John Harlow** (40) (AL) also lives in a household of several generations. His wife Charlotte (nee Marsh) (38) looks after a houseful of children. Thomas (11), Jessie (6) and Emily (5) all go to school while Alfred (3) and Charlotte (1) are at home. Charlotte's father **John Marsh** (63) also lives with them, but he still works as an agricultural labourer and is out of the house during the day. He first appeared in 1851, with his wife Ann and two daughters. However, he was widowed by the time of the 1861 census, after which he lived with his sister Sarah Spickett for a while.

## A Widowed Brother

**George Cork** (63) is a labourer on the parish roads and lives with his wife Elizabeth (69) and his brother Thomas Cork (66) (AL) who is now a widower. We have seen George on every census so far, and it has been interesting to follow his story through his two marriages and the birth of his children to his old age. He would now be wearing a fustian jacket instead of his old-fashioned smock, and have traded his moleskin trousers for ones made of corduroy.

## An Odd Mix

Listed next is an unusual mix of people. **Charles Reynolds** (32) (AL) lives with his wife Mary (25) and her daughter Mary Raines (4). Mary was unmarried at the time of her daughter's birth, as the child carries her mother's maiden name, not the name of her father. Also in the house is Emily Raines (12) who is listed as Charles' sister-in-law and thus must be Mary's sister.

## Trades and Professions

Those with trades and professions now proliferate

## On Bolts Hill:

### A Gardener

William Rains (34) who is a gardener and his wife Ellen (32) have recently moved to Shalmsford. They have one son, William, whose is just one month old. William has two jobs and also works as a domestic servant as demand dictates.

### A New Publican at 'The Cross Keys'

William Oldfield (37) and his wife Emily (29) are also new to the area. They have taken over 'The Cross Keys' pub and live there with their daughters Elizabeth (6), Ada (4),

The Cross Keys

Charlotte (2) and Alice (1). They also have their niece Mary Ashton (15) living with them and paying her keep by acting as a general servant. She would be expected to help with the housework, look after the children and possibly help in the pub as well. The girls were all born in the area, so I assume the couple moved here in the first half of the decade.

## A Teacher

**Philip Platten** (45) and his family have moved to Box Tree Cottages from Norfolk. He is listed as a teacher, and eventually becomes the Headmaster of Chartham Primary School, serving for 27 years. His wife Marian (40) is from Trowse in Norfolk, as is their son Herbie (16). Their daughter Gertie (12) was born in Gaywood in Norfolk, and this may indicate the moves Philip has made in order to find a good position. Herbie and Gertie are both still shown as scholars, despite their ages. Their lodger Eliza Taylor (55) is a widowed paper sorter and was born in Chartham.

## A Bricklayer

**William Boughton** (51) and his family are also new to the area and have moved to Box Tree Cottages. Their five-year-old son was born in Ashford, which was the last place they lived. This might either signify a new round of building in Bolts Hill, or that the original residents have moved on. William lives with his wife Charlotte (46) and their four boys Jesse (21), Alfred (19), Willie (13) and Thomas (5). William is a bricklayer and unlike the previous family, his boys are not at school. The two oldest sons are bricklayer's labourers. Willie is an agricultural labourer and Thomas is still at home. Thomas has been dumb since birth, and it is sad to note that by the time he is 16 he is in the Bridge Workhouse, listed as an 'idiot' and as a permanent resident rather than someone on temporary relief. As he grew up, his parents were unable to care for him any longer.

## A Shepherd

Also living in Box Trees cottages is Richard's son **James Mitchell Hoare** (42) who is a shepherd, and we saw him in Shalmsford Street in the 1851 census. He lives with his wife Emma (nee Mumford) (41) and four children Alfred (14), Elizabeth (9), Frederick (7) and Ellen (4). Alfred works with this father as a shepherd's boy, while the other children go to school.

Interestingly, Frederick is listed as having been born in America. James and Emma must have gone out with their family seeking a better life but returned within a very short time. The date of their sailing was after 1871, as Elizabeth was born in June. She is baptized on June 4th 1871.

There is also a parish record entry in 1863 for a baby called Ann, who was the child of James Mitchell and Emma Hoare. She was baptized on January 4th and went on to marry Henry Spillett.

This birth was followed the next year by that of Mitchell, baptized March 27th 1866, who died seven weeks later. Perhaps the death of these two children galvanised the couple to try to make a new life for themselves overseas.

James was seen but rarely in the village, as his work was out in the fields with his sheep, especially at lambing time, when he lived in a shepherd's hut, so as to be on hand even in the middle of the night. When he was seen, he was identified by his long shepherd's crook.

## A Papermaker

Near the Deanery, in Deanery Cottages is the household of **Thomas May** (51) a paper maker. He was born in Buckinghamshire, but his wife Ellen (nee Brazier)(32) was born in Maidstone and his children Ellen (3) Rhoda (2) and Gertrude (2 months) were all born in Chartham. Ellen is helped at home by **Harriet Sims** (13) who works as a general servant. Harriet's parents still live in Shalsmford Street. We saw Harriet at home in the 1871 census living in a rowdy house of sisters. I expect she is glad to get out during the day but happy to see them when she returns home in the evenings.

## A Policeman

Lastly in Box Tree Cottages is William Stoner (58) from Cuckfield in Sussex, who has moved here with his wife Martha (40). He is one of the two local police officers. Their three eldest children William (8), Alice (6) and Emily (4) all go to school, while Edith (2) is still at home. William wore a police-issue greatcoat and carried a baton, a lantern and a rattle.

## A Gardener

Also in Deanery Cottages is **Cornelius Sudds** (38), a gardener from Mereworth with his wife Rosa (28) and their children Harry (5), William (4) and Alfred (3). The children were all born in Chartham, so I can assume the family has been here five or six years. Cornelius also works as a domestic servant, either out-of-season or at the whim of his employer. His two older boys both attend school.

## A Groom and Milkman

In Court Lodge cottages is **Thomas Ellen** (29) who is a groom and milkman. He has moved here from Shepherdswell with his wife Sarah Ann (27) and their daughter Jane (8). Their son William (6) was born in Chartham. Both children are listed as scholars.

## Working at The Paper Mill

Another family who have moved into the area after they were married is the Cox family who live near the Deanery. **Thomas Cox** (33) and Elizabeth Cox (28) were both born outside the area, but their children Albert (4), William (3) and Mabel (10 months) were all born in Chartham. They live with Elizabeth's mother **Mercy Wheeler** (75) who is now widowed. Thomas works as a labourer at the paper mill.

### A Farmer

At Court Lodge Farm is George Coltham (76) is a farmer of 74 acres, employing one man. He was born in Elham and his housekeeper, Eliza Boatwright (67) was born in Reculver, and they are new to the area. It is not clear which farm he has taken over.

At the time of the census George was not to know that he would suffer a set-back in the summer of 1883. One of his straw stacks was set on fire and he suffered a loss of about £30. The local newspaper report says the Mr Stoner, who lived in Box Tree cottages, worked 'indefatigably' to put it out, ensuring that 'water was poured plentifully onto the fire' until it was out.'

### A Retired Publican

**Thomas Newington** (80) has now retired and moved out of 'The Cross Keys' to Box Trees House. He still lives in Box Trees with his wife Ann (73) and his daughter **Amelia Rudduck** (56) along with their granddaughter Elizabeth Rudduck (19), but granddaughter Amy has moved on. New to the household is Ann's brother **John Court** (75), who is now a widower and retired steward of antiquities. Amelia and Elizabeth both teach at the board school, which was opened in 1872.

### A Sweet Shop Keeper

**Elizabeth Dixon** was shown in 1871 living with her husband James and daughter Mercy. She is now widowed but still lives near the Deanery. As her 1871 address was Deanery Cottages, I assume she has not moved. She earns a living as a sweet shop keeper.

## Shalmsford Street

### Four Carpenters

William Ruck (41) is a carpenter and lives with his wife Maria (nee Smith) (44). His five children are William (21), a bricklayer's labourer, Lavinia (14), Benjamin (11), Marie (or Maud) (5) and Fred (3). The whole family were born in Chartham. We see William Jnr in the next census as head of his own household.

Benjamin Norris Pay (33) was born in Chartham, as were his wife and children. He works as a carpenter, while his wife Elizabeth (nee Clark) (30) looks after the house and their four children. Benjamin is 6 and goes to school, whereas James (4), Walter (3) and Mary Ann (9 months) are still at home. We first saw Benjamin on the 1851 census, where he is shown at just 3 years old living with his parents in Shalmsford Street.

William Bangham (44) is still also in Shalmsford Street with his wife Mary Ann

(40) and is a carpenter. Mary looks after their daughter Clara (3).

William Wells (38) was born in Bishopsbourne, a few miles south of Chartham, and has married Mary (41) from Woolwich. William works as a rough farm carpenter and sawyer and Mary is a charwoman. Their oldest daughter Jane (19), who works as a nurse to younger children, was born in Bishopsbourne. The couple's second daughter Sarah (15) works as a general servant, and the last three, Thomas (10), Mary (7) and Edwin (5) all go to school.

## A Plumber

**Thomas Streeting** (45) is now a master plumber and glazier and lives with his wife Eliza (45) and two of their children, Arthur (14) and Walter (13). Both boys attend school. Their oldest boy Thomas is now 20 and has left home.

## At the Paper Mill

Listed next to them, but not necessarily living next door is **William Page** (27), from East Malling who works as a paper maker in the Chartham paper mill. He lives with his wife Emma (23) who was born in Woolwich. I wonder if Mary is Emma's mother? They moved here when William was offered his job at the mill as both children, Alice (2) and William (4 months) were born in Chartham. **Eliza Page** (24) lives with them and works as a housemaid. She is from West Malling, again showing the distance new residents travel to get here.

**Maria Vincer** (61) is an old friend. We have seen her family on every census return so far. She still works, and is a paper sorter at the mill. She lives with her daughters Elizabeth (36) and Ann (17) as well as Frances Vincer, (6) who is Elizabeth's daughter. While Frances is at school, Elizabeth and Ann accompany their mother to the mill, where Elizabeth is a rag worker and Ann is a paper sorter.

Rag sorters divided the newly-arrived rags into types, whether linen, cotton etc., and into colour, before they were cut and processed into paper. Each type needed to undergo a slightly different process, e.g. longer in the pulper, so they needed to be kept separate. The women would also have been expected to remove any buttons etc. from the clothing.

## A Carter

**Frederick Ford** (31) is new to the area. His wife Selina (30) was born in Poplar, in the East End of London, a very poor area at this time. Frederick works as a carter, while Selina is a bavin chopper. The two eldest children Elizabeth (9) and Frederick (4) go to school, while Emily (1) is at home. This leads to the conclusion that Selina works from home, although she may take Emily along with her while she works outdoors. There are several other bavin workers in Shalmsford Street, so they may have arranged an informal crèche system amongst themselves.

## Working with Wood

The next family in the enumerator's book is that of **Richard Baldock** (36). Richard is a carrier and wood dealer but his wife Emma (36) has no occupation listed. His two eldest daughters Eliza (16) and Kate (14) are bavin choppers. It could well be that Richard employs the other ladies in the street who do the same work. The couple's next two daughters Ann (10) and Jane (5) go to school and the youngest two, Jane (3) and Matilda (4 months) are at home. This would explain why Emma has no time for an occupation apart from looking after the home and family.

It is a sad reflection of the times that Ann was sent home from school several times in 1881 for having nits in her hair.

**Edward Hoare** (34) works as a woodman and general labourer to support his wife Harriett (33) and his five children. The oldest three children Harriet (10), William (9) and Walter (6) all attend school, while Minnie (3) and Frederick (2) are too young yet. We first met Edward and Harriett when they were living with their respective parents in 1861. They were married by 1871 and have stayed in the area. This family may live in 3 Fern Cottages, now part of 81 Shalmsford Street.

**Henry Spillett**, nephew to Edward SPillett, (50) is a wood dealer. He and his wife Sophia (47) have adopted a girl called **Mary A. Hoare**, who is now five and attends school. Sophie's maiden name was Hoare, so it is probable that she is a relative. They also have a lodger in the house: **Edward Thompsett** (19) a carter to the coal merchant.

**John Gibson** (42) works as a hurdle maker. His wife Harriet (44) has the maiden name of Hoare, and she is George's daughter. The couple's oldest sons John (22) and George (16) work as agricultural labourers, while the younger boy James (3) recorded as a scholar. In reality, he will be staying at home with his mother during the day. The Gibsons have also listed George Hoare (9) who is their nephew, and who is also a scholar.

John is cousin to James Mitchell Hoare, and they worked closely together, as good quality, transportable hurdles were invaluable to the shepherd. He might even have worked in the fields with James during busy times, mending and maintaining fences.

## Working On the Railway

It is reported that one in five men rely on the railway for work, from platelaying to engine-driving or in one of the associated trades such as using horse-drawn vehicles to transport goods and passengers to and from the railway stations, and the manufacture of carts and wagons which gives work to local wheelwrights and blacksmiths.

**John Catt** (23) from Ebony, Kent has married Edward Pay's daughter Mary (22). John works as a porter on the railway and Mary has her hands full with William, their one month old son.

**Joseph Oliver** (54), a platelayer on the South Eastern railway and his wife Elizabeth (45) have moved her from Great Chart, just outside Ashford. They have a family of eight at home, consisting of Arthur (18), Frederick (14), Emily (11), David (11), Stephen (6), Charlie (6), Lucy (4) and Edmund (1). Arthur brings in a wage as a bricklayer's labourer, Frederick works as a farm house boy and all the other children except little Edmund go to school. What a relief it must be to Elizabeth when the school bell rings!

**William Hazelwood** (39) is from Thetford in Cambridgeshire and has married Kentish girl Jane (32) from Bethersden. They live with their sons William (7) and Frederic (sic)(5) who both go to school. William works as a platelayer on the railway.

Joseph's son **Richard Oliver** (22) is also a platelayer on the railway. He has recently married Ann (19) from Blean and they have a one-year-old son, Henry. A platelayer is someone who lays and maintains railway track. Once a railway was built by contractors, the railway company employed platelayers who worked in gangs under a 'ganger' or foreman. The work was undertaken between the passing of trains, so the track was not closed to traffic during the work. Each gang was responsible for the maintenance of a particular length, and the work was sought after by local men not only because the pay was higher than agricultural work, but also because the men were on permanent contract, unaffected by seasonal labour requirements.

**George Epps** (53) is a platelayer on the London, Chatham & Dover (LCD) Railway, originally from Wye. He lives with his wife Maria (57) and **Emily Fraser** (9) who is from Rainham in Essex. The LCD line runs a third of a mile north of Shalmsford, passing through Chartham Hatch on its way to Canterbury.

We met **Mary Stacey** (50) in 1861 as the wife of Obediah Solomon, living at the Railway Gate House. When he died, she married James Stacey, a labourer. We now see her back at the Railway Gate House again, as James (49) now works as a Platelayer on the South Eastern Railway. Jane Solomon (24) is the child of her first marriage and Mary (17) and James (15) are James' children. All three younger members of the family work as glaziers in the paper mill. Having four good incomes would make this an affluent household in Shalmsford Street terms.

## Shoemakers and Menders

**Jesse Hoare** (58), shoemaker, is a familiar face. He is now widowed and bringing up a family of five, with the help of his daughter who is listed as a housekeeper.

The children are: Harry (18), Emily (16), William (9), Jesse (7) and Rosa (3). Annie is working elsewhere. Jesse's wife Louisa has only recently passed away, and he still gives his marital state as 'married' rather than 'widower'. However, he marries Jane Pay in 1882, and we see him living with his extended family on the next census. Harry works as a bricklayer's labourer.

One anomaly is that Jesse had a son called George who should be listed on this census aged 9, but instead we see William. William appears to be his nephew, son of Edward and Harriet Hoare. Jesse's son George is with his own aunt and uncle on the night of the census, John and Harriet Gibson.

## A Groom

We follow a run of newcomers, as next on the list is **William Neame** (25) and his wife Emily (23) who is from Dover. William is out of the house working as a groom, while their oldest William (4) goes to school. Emily is at home with the two youngest children, Amy (2) and Sydney (4 months). Interestingly, William was born in Maidstone, which again shows how much people moved around in search of work. I don't know where William works, but it will be in one of the local pubs or farmhouses, possible 'The George'; he was on call at any time, so would need to live near to where he worked.

## A Gamekeeper

Yet another new family is that of **Harry Radley** (57), his wife Annie (34) and their two daughters Louisa (3) and Alice (1). None of this family were born in the area, but Annie comes from Woodnesborough near Sandwich. Harry works as a gamekeeper although he is currently out of work. He moves around to find work as the children were born in Brightlingsea, Sussex and Marden, Kent.

## A Milkman and a Gardener

**John W. Daniels** (34) appeared as a boarder on the 1871 census. He is now married to Clara (nee Jordan) (27) and works as a milkman and gardener. Clara was born in Chilham, as was John, and they no doubt knew each other from childhood. The children were all born in Chartham: Walter (7), Joseph (4), Mary Ann (2) and Frank (1).

**George Burchett** (70) is also a long-standing resident of Shalmsford Street and still lives in the area called Loampits. We met him in 1851, when he and his family lived with his parents. He has continued the family tradition of keeping the family together and now lives in the family home with his own son Ambrose (28) and his wife Jane (Alice Jane Collard)(23). Ambrose' son Arthur is only one month old.

Both men work as boot makers, which is a benefit of living in a rural community. Many boot and shoe makers in the cities have seen their trade cut dramatically since the introduction of mechanisation in the industry.

## Two Nurses

We saw **Henry Cork** (34) (AL) in the last census with a wife and young family. He has continued to live in the area and must find it frustrating to see his boys have to go to school at an age when he was out at work. His wife Esther (35) is from Lynsted. The children are George (11), Jane (10) and Frederick (7). They have been joined in their household by **Ann Holness** (72) who is employed as a nurse to Esther, while her occupation is 'pauper from the union' (workhouse). It may be that she works for her board only. She was born in Hampshire. The nature of Esther's illness is not given, but it is possibly be due to a complication in pregnancy as she is well within child-bearing age and I would expect to see further children after Frederick, who is now 7.

**Mary Barker** (78) is listed as a pauper, but she is the head of her household. This is the same Mary we saw on Bolts Hill in 1841. Her daughter Eliza (35) now has two children, who appear to be illegitimate as they have not taken their father's name: Gertrude Barker (9) and Emily Barker (5). The both go to school while Eliza works as a monthly nurse, assisting new mothers in the first weeks of their baby's life.

## A Labourer on the Parish Roads

**Alfred Warden** (26) was born in Chartham and married Emily (nee Greenstreet) (22) in 1881 They have one son, Frederick, (8 months). Alfred works as a labourer on the parish roads. This was back-breaking work. Women, children and the elderly would work in the fields to clear stones that would otherwise blunt the plough shares. These stones would then be carted to the site of the road repairs where they were used to strengthen (or metal) the road. This would then be covered with grit or gravel. Another aspect of the work was creating or maintaining the ditches that ran on either side of the cambered road to keep them clear.

The family thrive, however, as I find a baptism record for Frances Anne dated September 4th 1887, on which her parents, Alfred and Emma are listed as living in Bolts Hill, with the husband's occupation being victualler.

## Two Bricklayers

We first saw **James Vidgen** on 1861 as a nine-year-old living with his parents

Edward and Charlotte. He is now 29 and head of his own household, working as a bricklayer. His wife Emily (nee Hoare) (29) has recently given birth to their daughter Ethel (6 months) who is sister to William (3), but she is dead by the end of this year.

**Henry Cork** (58) also works as a bricklayer and lives with his wife Jane (54) and four of his children. His son Edward (17) helps in the business, as his occupation is given as bricklayers assistant. Son John (14) is recorded as a general labourer, but this is probably in his father's business as well. The two youngest children Charles (12) and Jesse (9) are at school.

Young John is destined to travel the world, as I found when I looked at the 1901 census:

John Cork (34) is a bricklayer with a large family. His wife Dorcas (33) from Yalding has recently given birth to their youngest child, Frank who is just 6 months old. The other children are Dorcas (12), John (8), Violet (7) and Fred (1). It is astonishing to see that most of the children were born in Chartham, and Dorcas Laura was born in Chilham, but the place of birth for Violet Mabel clearly says New York, USA. This is confirmed by her 1911 return, which carries a note beside her place of birth saying 'British subject by parentage'.

Further investigation shows an immigration record for Dorcas Cork, age 26, leaving from Southampton and arriving in New York on 6th October 1893, the year before Violet's birth, but I can find no record of the family's return. However, they must have been back here by 1899, when Fred's birth is registered in Chartham.

## Publican at 'The George'

**James Stupples** (45) from Elmstead now manages 'The George' with his wife Jane (43) who is from Denton. Their son Henry (20) also helps in the business. They have two daughters, Rose (7) and Minnie (5) who go to school and one general servant, **Elizabeth Gordon** (18). Also in the house is a lodger, **William Barker** (25)(AL).

James may have been instrumental in pursuing the road improving road improvements near 'The George', as the road between 'The George' and Shalmsford Bridge was raised in the 1880s so that it was above flood level.

## A Blacksmith

**George Kingsland** (29) has moved into Shalmsford Street since the last census with his wife Jane (27). George is a master blacksmith and is training James Cullen (13) in the craft. James lives with George and Jane but is apprenticed to H. Smith rather than to George, although you would generally expect an apprentice to live in. Jane looks after her own one-year-old child Winifred and also has care of **Ernest Fullager** (3) who is described as a nurse child. A nurse child was generally an illegitimate or otherwise unwanted child who was fostered by another family. Ernest was back with his mother by the time of the next survey.

## Two Laundresses

**William Gibson** (53) is a general labourer and his wife Elizabeth, a laundress, is the same age. Their daughter **Rosa Baines** lives with them, and she works with Elizabeth as a laundress. The washing was brought to their house, where they wash, dry and iron it before returning it to the owner. **Mabel Gibson** (8) also lives here, and is Rosa's child from before her marriage – I found a baptism record for Mabel Ellen Gibson dated March 27th 1873 with Rose Ennis Gibson as her mother.

## The Farm Bailiff

**Edward Spillett** (72) works as a farm bailiff and lives with his daughter Mary (27) who gives her occupation as housekeeper. Edward is the father of several of the Shalmsford inhabitants, but I have been unable to place Mary. He was seen around the village in a tall 'billycock' hat, which was like a tall top hat, the height of which indicated the length of service.

## A Master Builder

**John Wood** (57) is a master builder employing 11 men and 5 boys. He lives with his wife Anne (41) and his stepdaughter Emma Mumford (13). Emma still goes to school. Anne was married to her previous husband, a miller for only four years before he died, after which she moved back home with her parents in Lower Ensign Farm before marrying John in 1873.

## A River Watcher

**William Hoare** (25) is a river watcher. His wife Emma (nee Down) (25) looks after their first child Robert (1). William's job, working for the Customs Service, is to watch the river and check for ships/barges unloading any cargo that had tax payable upon it. The job was later changed to Revenue Assistant.

## Carpenters and Wheelwrights

**William Ralph** (31) is also from Canterbury and works as a carpenter. His wife Fanny (29) was born in Llanwally, and I wonder how she came to be living in Kent, as far away from Monmouthshire in Wales as it is possible to go. Their son George (9 months old) was born in Chartham.

**Robert Cruttenden** (27) from Teynham is a wheelwright and carpenter and was been welcomed to the area. Carts and wagons were still in use on a daily basis, although machinery had begun to sneak into larger farms on the larger fields. Wagons made in Kent were recognised by their shapes – they had waisted bodies and straight sides, with about a dozen flat spars either side, giving a boxy rather than a fluid shape. Kentish wagons were painted with a distinctive scarlet under-carriage.

Roberts wife Mary (23) was born in Canterbury, and their first child William (1) has just been born.

**Charles Nesbit Gibson** (34), a carpenter, has also taken an elderly relative into his home. He is from Rye and his wife Sarah (35) was born in Shadoxhurst. Their children are Evelyn (10), George (8) and Alice (5) who all attend school. Sarah's mother **Mary Martin** (79) is the widow of a farmer.

## A Charwoman

**Mary Rumley** (50) works as a charwoman, hired by the day to do odd jobs (usually cleaning), and as a widow is now head of her family. One imagines her to be a formidable woman. She is mother to five boys George (19), George (16), William (15), Charles (13) and Edward (11). After my initial thought that this must be a rowdy household, I notice that all the boys are out during the day. This is the reason Mary is able to work. George is a general labourer at the paper mill, Edward is at school and the other boys are agricultural labourers. Despite the low wages of the time with five of the six occupants of the house working, they were considerably better off than many of their neighbours. This is in stark contrast to the previous fortunes of the family. The 1871 census shows the whole family, including father George in the Ashford workhouse. His grave, in Chartham churchyard, shows that he diee in 1875, so perhaps he was too ill to work and support his large family (six children were recorded with him in the workhouse as well as his wife). In 1861 he had been living in Rattington Street, Chartham with Mary and his first child, Elizabeth. I have not been able to trace either Elizabeth or her brother Alfred after the appeared on the workhouse returns aged 7 and 5.

I have been unable to fathom the reason for Mary having two sons called George. The only explanation is that one of them is NOT her son. It may be a mistake by the enumerator, or she might have adopted a child, possibly someone she met in the workhouse that she claimed was hers so he was released with her.

## A Certified Schoolmistress

**Henry Cook** (52) lives with his wife Charlotte (49) and his two children. He works as a general labourer and Arthur (7) is still at school.

George's oldest girl, Lydia (25) works as an assistant certified mistress at the Board School. To become certified she was tested in grammar, geography, history, math, and writing from dictation as well as handwriting style. After the Education Act of 1870, school teachers were trained at teacher-pupil centres and sent for work experience in schools. Lydia will be one of the first teachers to be trained in this way and earnt about £75 per year, according to Cassell's Household Guide.

Ten years earlier, 15-year-old Lydia had been employed as a Monitor at the school, teaching infants under the supervision of the teacher, cleaning the school, lighting the fires and taking charge of the school during the dinner hour.

## Two Carters

**Henry Amos** (59) has now returned to Shalmsford Street with his wife Francis (64). We previously saw them in 1851. In 1861 and 1871 he worked as a carter at the Corn Mill, where they lived. They now share their home with **Isabella Wood** (22) who works as a nurse and is the wife of a sailor in the Royal Navy and was born in Berwick-upon-Tweed. She has a daughter, one-year old Gertrude. It is not clear whether she works as a nurse somewhere outside the home, or whether she cares for Francis, who I know dies later this year. It is possible she works at the County Asylum which was opened recently. Henry works as a builder's carter, a step up from his previous work as an agricultural labourer.

**John Fagg** (26) was born in Canterbury as is a carter, who drives a wagon, usually with two horses. His wife Catherine (24) was born in Elham and his older child John was born in Thanington. Only their baby, Frank (9 months), was born in Chartham, suggesting that they have only lived here for a few years.

## The Life Insurance Salesman

**Albert Naish** (23) earns his living as a commissioned agent selling life insurance. He comes from Newport, but his wife Ellen (22) and his young son Cuthbert (6 months) were born in Surbiton. Perhaps he met them on his travels around the country selling door to door.

## Two Gardeners

**John Link** (47) still lives with his wife Ann (62). He is now a gardener/domestic servant while Ann works as a laundress.

**Joseph Stubberfield** (68) is still a gardener, nurseryman and sodsman. He lives with his wife Harriet (67) and his daughter Mary Ann (32). We have watched this family since our first look at the 1841 census, but sadly, Joseph is dead by the 1891 census.

## A Policeman

**Edwin Martin** (34) is the local police constable. He lives with his wife Annie (27) and their three children. Robert (3), Henry (2) and Eliza (11 months) were all born in Chartham.

## A Builder

**Alfred Foreman** (55) lives with his wife Jane (50) and they live with three servants, **Rosa Moat** (18), **Henry Evans** (17) and **Alfred Oldfield** (25). Their son Frank has now left home. He is a master builder employing four men and seven lads.

## An Attendant at the Lunatic Asylum

**Jesse Collier** (52), a Head Attendant at the Lunatic Asylum. His wife Sarah (44) was born in Rochester, Kent, and Jesse was born in Buckinghamshire.

## Bricklayers and Labourers

Next we see the familiar faces of **Tritton Adams** (55) and his family. Firstly, is his wife Rebecca, who juggles the household while Tritton is at work as a bricklayer. Next is their daughter Harriet (21), who married James Link, a stoker on the railway, but is now staying with them either for the night of the census or permanently. She has come with her daughter **Ellie Link** (1). Also in the house are Rebecca's widowed father **John Fraser** (78) who is not working, but still proudly puts his occupation as 'agricultural labourer out of employ' and **Rose Sanden** (12), the couple's niece from Pevensey, Kent. She is recorded as a scholar. John undoubtedly still picks up odd days of work in season.

Curiously, there is a Situations Wanted advert in The Hastings and St Leonards Observer in April 1883, in which James Link of Shalmsford Street asks for work as a Stoker and Driver. He was away at the time of the 1881 census looking for work and he may be the same James Link who was a stoker on the HMS Druid. Some sources say that he is the same James Link who emigrated to America in 1888 with his family and lived there with his wife until his death.

**Sarah Hoare** (63) gives her occupation as 'wife of ag lab'. She lives with her sons Frederick Hoare (23) and John Hoare (15) now her husband John has passed away. Frederick is a bricklayer and John is a bricklayer's labourer. Her husband was John, brother to George and Richard, and her son Edward and daughter Emily still live in Shalmsford, having married James Vidgen and his sister Sarah, respectively.

## A Needlewoman

**Sarah Burchett** (63) supports herself by working as a needlewoman and by taking in a lodger. Her lodger is **Richard Mumford** (18) who we saw previously living with his parents. He is now a bricklayer's labourer.

## Shalmsford Farm House

**John Gambrill** (55) still lives at Shalmsford Farm House and looks after the farm of 150 acres, employing 4 men and 1 boy. He is still married to Catherine (50). Their children are Sidney (19), Mary (18), Sarah (11), Lucy (9) and Susan (5). Several of Catherine's relatives now live with the family. The house is large enough for **Mary Allen** (74), Catherine's mother (widow of a butcher), Elizabeth Allen (40) her sister (a barmaid out of employ), and Florie Allen (24), a general servant who is listed as John's stepdaughter. This would make her

Catherine's daughter from before her marriage, as her maiden name is Allen. One gets the impressions that Elizabeth and Florie are playing on Catherine's good nature to stay at the farmhouse while not earning an income. Also in the house are two servants, **William Epps** (19) and **Solomon Brice** (18) who work as carters/agricultural labourers.

## A Labourer

**Thomas Cavell Newton** (33) supports a large family on his wages as a general labourer. His wife Jane (nee Link) (29) does not work and his oldest child Frederick Charles is only (8), so is in school. His other son, Henry is one year old. In the last census we saw Jane at age 19 living with her father and working in the paper mill, so life has changed dramatically for her over the last ten years. Thomas has given a home to his mother-in-law **Jane Link** (71) who is now widowed and his niece **Florence Myhurst**, who is still at school. Jane's mother is recorded as a pauper, which shows she has no income and is supported by Thomas.

## Butcher and Grocer

**George Elvey** (24) is recorded as a butcher and grocer. He is now head of the household and he is the primary wage-earner for his extended family. He lives with his father Benjamin (60), his mother Betsey (58) and his niece **Hephzibah Wraight** (10), who goes to school locally. She is the daughter of George's sister Betsey. Benjamin gives his occupation as 'mariner' but at 60 he will now be retired. If he was in the Royal Navy he will be in receipt of a pension and listed as a pensioner.

Shops at this time opened from 8am until 8pm, with late opening on a Friday until 10pm or later, to allow people the opportunity to spend their weekly wages.

It is confusing to note in the parish records that George Elvey and his wife Ellen brought their son Charles Benjamin to the church on January 15th to be welcomed by baptism. Maybe both are away visiting now Charles is four months old and can travel.

## A Retired Couple

**John Homersham** and his wife Elizabeth are now both 67 years old. John has no longer works and has saved enough money for a comfortable retirement. The couple have one servant, **Ellen Edwards** (15).

## No Pension for Thomas

**Thomas Bartlett** (70) is a widower and now lives on his own. He was born in Chartham and still works as a woodman.

## The Landlady

**Sophia Henshaw** (65) is a widow from Ringstead in Northamptonshire is the head of her household of one. She takes in two boarders, **Richard Pay** (45) who previously boarded with the Webbs, and

**Edward Page** who is only 6. Sophia works as a bavin wood chopper, Richard is an agricultural labourer and Edward goes to school. If the enumerator's handwriting was not so perfectly neat, I would suspect that Page was a mis-translation of Pay and that the two boarders were related, but this does not seem to be the case.

## Three Paupers

**John Young** (61) still lives on his own, but is now a pauper. Further, he is noted as being 'almost blind' on the census return.

**John Adams** (82) is also recorded as being a pauper, by which he means he has no income. He lives with his grandsons William (17) and James (13). William supports all three of them with his wages from the paper mill.

**Ann Pay** (74) is now a widow and also lives on her own as a pauper. We first met Ann in 1851 when she lived with her husband and young family. We have seen the family grow and leave home, and husband James pass away. We can only assume that her children still live in the area and help to support her to remain living independently in her own home.

## Two Grocers and a Coal Merchant

**Alfred Stockbridge** (46) is a grocer and coal merchant who was born in Petham. His wife Ann (43) was born in the same village. They live with their two nieces **Annie Harris** (11) and **Ada Uden** (16) who both go to school. Neither were born in Chartham, although Harris and Uden are both local names.

**George Homersham** (34) has taken over his father's business and is a grocer and coal merchant employing one man and a boy. The shop was been one of the central meeting points of the village. No doubt his wife Elizabeth (nee Wells) (32) helps in the shop, chatting as she does so. They have one servant to help with the work, **Emily Lewis** (16). Also in the house are two of Elizabeth's cousins. **Fanny Wells** (18), a telegraphist and **Frederick Wells** (14) who is, unsurprisingly, a grocer's assistant. George and Elizabeth have been married since 1775, but have no children of their own. It is sad to consider that George dies in 1886. Elizabeth marries James Nash in 1888 and lives until 1927.

## A Sailor's Wife

**Ann Jennings** (24) is married, but lives on her own. Her husband is in The Royal Navy, so is away for long periods at a time.

## A Dealer in Horse Flesh

It is interesting to note that a large, extended family (below) is recorded in caravans in Shalmsford Street. As the road had not extended much above the Bolts Hill turning at this date, these could have been either at the top or the bottom of the road, but it is likely that they were camped near 'The George'.

**John Ransley** (50) is head of a large family and is a horse dealer. His wife Celia is also 50. They have two unmarried sons, John (12) and Richard (7) and two married daughters. The first daughter is Sarah (27) who has married Frederic (sic) Tansy (26). They have three children, John (8), James (6) and Walter (2). The second daughter is Phoebe (22) who has married Henry Beaney (22) and has one child, John (1).

This decade saw an expansion in the clothing market, with machine-made clothing in bright new chemical colours becoming readily available to young women, so I hope Sarah and Phoebe found enough money to enjoy this phenomenon.

Number 63 Shalmsford Street, build in 1717, was once known as Ransley's Farm, and it was probably the home of this family.

As with the previous years, there are several people who have slipped through the net of the census. Some of those I have been able to track down by looking at other historical documents.

One of the interesting tales from Shalmsford is that of a missing child who

lived in Shalmsford Street in 1882. She is the daughter of Mr Sladden, and the family moved in soon after the censu

The report tells us that Mr Sladden reported his daughter stolen when she failed to return home after a Saturday visit to the fair in Canterbury with friends. Luckily, the child had met and

gone home with her aunt and uncle and turned up home safe and sound on the following Wednesday, but the tone of the report suggests that the police were not amused at the amount of time spent looking for the child and printing placards, when she was not ever truly lost.

# The 1890s

The 1890s continued with the same weather that had plagued the 1800s. Snowy winters became the norm and rainfall was considerably reduced. February 1895 saw the Great Frost when even The Thames and The Medway were frozen, and temperatures fell to the lowest ever recorded. Outdoor work was impossible. In 1893 saw only 30% of the expected rainfall culminating in a heat wave in 1899.

Lives were improving amongst the poor of the village since the introduction of legislation for landlords concerning sanitation, ventilation and light, although life was still hard for the lowest paid individuals.

However, life in general was still hard for those living in rural locations such as Shalmsford. The roads were still in a poor state, and street lighting had not yet been introduced, cooking was done over a wood-fired stove and sanitation was still basic.

1891 saw the abolition of the 'school penny', which was the fee for attending school. After this date, the school claimed ten shillings per child per year. A change to the school day was that the school leaving age was raised to 11 in 1893 and to 12 in 1899, which had had a serious impact on those families who relied on the earning of their children to make ends meet. However, many children still did not attend school, because of the continuing need for them to be working to help support the family.

An article in the local paper gives us an insight into the housing of Shalmsford Street. It is reported that Mr Baldock paid £435 for three cottages in Shalmsford Street and that the rental was £31 and 4 shillings. There is no Mr Baldock living in Shalmsford at this time, so he is a landlord, buying property specifically to rent out. I wonder if these were Myrtle Cottages?

The Easter of 1894 brought excitement to the village. The South London Brigade of Volunteers came to Canterbury for a long weekend of exercises and on Saturday the Cyclists and Mounted Infantry came to Shalmsford to see how well they could defend the west side of Canterbury from attack, as reported in The Whitstable and Herne Bay Herald dated 31st March 1894.

The Inns of Court Mounted Infantry with the 26th Middlesex Cycling Corp and the Artists Cycling Section took up position in Shalmsford Street under Captain Liles while the Queens Westminster Mounted Infantry with their own Cyclist Section, the Civil Service and the 2nd Middlesex formed ranks in Chilham under Lieutenant Tottie.

Operations commenced at 11.30am and Lt. Tottie's Cyclists were 'beaten back' by those of Capt. Liles. He then brought out the Mounted Infantry, who drove the defending Cyclists back to Chartham, while Capt. Liles held Shalmsford Street with the rest of his force.

After a one-hour break for lunch, Capt. Liles reformed at a strong position between Horton and Milton and held off the attacking force until 4pm, when the ceasefire was sounded. It sounds like a good time was had by all, not least the Shalmsford villagers.

This same year the children enjoyed an extended summer, due to the extension of the harvest period; the holiday in 1894 lasted eleven weeks!

Further festivities were seen in the village in June 1897, when Alfred Foreman once again gave a party to celebrate Queen Victoria's Diamond Jubilee, this time for The Queen's Golden Jubilee. He invited the young people of the village aged 14-20 to attend a garden party, and 49 enjoyed a sit-down tea on the lawn. Tenants and friends joined them in the evening, when they played croquet and other lawn games, to the musical accompaniment of Miss Jessie Nash of the piano.

The children and anyone who could snatch a spare half an hour would also have enjoyed visiting the fete on Chartham Village Green, which was decorated with Chinese lanterns and 200 flags. The children were presented with medals and brooches to mark the occasion, which were commissioned locally, possibly via private funding. A 'meat tea' was provide for the elderly; 60 ate in the school hall and 20 more, presumably those less mobile, were provided with tea in their own homes. There was a bonfire in the evening, and music from the St Stephen's Drum and Pipe Band. 200 prizes were distributed to the children, and many sought out high ground to get a look at the Diamond Jubilee Beacons which spanned the country as a sign of unity.

## 1891 Census

The 1891 census recorded the members of each household on the night of 5th April 1891. The local enumerator was George Norris. George already holds several positions in the village, having been appointed as the School Attendance Officer in 1888, and serving as Assistant Overseer of the Parish.

Shalmsford still falls within Enumeration District 2 comprises 'All the remaining part of Chartham, being that on the south east side of the River Stour. Contents: comprising Longneck, Mystole, Underdown, Perry Farm and cottages, Asylum cottages, Owls Home, Horton Chapel and cottages, Rattington Street, Court Lodge, Box Trees, Bolts Hill, Shalmsford Street and Pickledon'. 'Owls Home' was a local name for Upper Horton Farm.

The demographic in terms of age has now stabilized, with the number of children under the age of 10 (126) staying almost the same, as well as the number of older people, aged 70-80 (21). There are now 111 households recorded in the village, from Shalmsford Bridge to the site of Chartham Surgery, where Parish Road crosses the Stour.

This is the first census on which our old friend the 'ag lab' has been of such insignificant numbers that I have not included a separate category. Although Shalmsford is still undeniably a rural area (as it still is today) farming practices no longer seem to need a general agricultural labourer. This could be due to changes in land use as well as the introduction of machinery. Many who previously have described themselves as labourers have now taken on job titles such as woodreeve or rough carpenter, so I have aggregated such occupations under the one heading.

Occupations in Shalmsford, 1891

| Agricultural labourer | 66 | 30% |
|---|---|---|
| Labourer | 16 | 7% |
| Blacksmith | 13 | 6% |
| Domestic servant | 12 | 5% |
| Worker at the paper mill | 11 | 5% |
| Seamstress/dressmaker | 8 | 4% |
| Bricklayer | 5 | 2% |
| Teacher | 5 | 2% |
| Baker | 4 | 2% |
| Bricklayer's labourer | 4 | 2% |
| Carpenter | 4 | 2% |
| Housekeeper | 4 | 2% |
| Paper maker | 4 | 2% |
| Shop assistant | 4 | 2% |
| Wheelwright | 4 | 2% |
| Butcher | 3 | 1% |
| Farm bailiff | 3 | 1% |
| Gardener | 3 | 1% |
| Laundress | 3 | 1% |
| Salvation Army | 3 | 1% |
| Apprentice | 2 | 1% |
| Carter | 2 | 1% |
| Coal merchant | 2 | 1% |
| Engine driver | 2 | 1% |
| Farmer | 2 | 1% |
| Grocer | 2 | 1% |
| Miller | 2 | 1% |
| P.C. | 2 | 1% |
| Platelayer | 2 | 1% |
| Publican | 2 | 1% |
| Worker at the asylum | 2 | 1% |
| Builder | 1 | <1% |
| Chimney sweep | 1 | <1% |
| Engine fitter | 1 | <1% |
| Groom | 1 | <1% |
| Haberdasher | 1 | <1% |
| House painter | 1 | <1% |
| Insurance agent | 1 | <1% |
| Millwright | 1 | <1% |
| Nurse | 1 | <1% |
| Railway gate keeper | 1 | <1% |

| River keeper | 1 | <1% |
| --- | --- | --- |
| Shoemaker | 1 | <1% |
| Stoker and engine driver | 1 | <1% |
| Surgeon | 1 | <1% |
| Tailor | 1 | <1% |
| Water bailiff | 1 | <1% |
| Woodreeve | 1 | <1% |
| | 218 | |

The average wage of the agricultural labourer, which is still the major occupational group in the village, despite national trends to the contrary, would have earnt little more than he did at the beginning of Victoria's reign. His weekly wage was around 13s a week, a rise of about 50%, and he was still struggling to make ends meet. With his dark clothing very much like of the townsfolk and his flat cap, the 'ag. lab' looked very much like the working class man of the twentieth century, very different from the smock-wearing, highly-skilled countryman we met in 1841.

## Agricultural Labourers

### Shalmsford Street

**William Wells** (49) (AL) is still in Shalmsford Street with his wife Mary (52), but she is now calling herself Maria. The only child they now have at home is Edward (previously transcribed as Edwin) (15), who is an agricultural labourer, so they are able to enjoy their 4 rooms.

Our friend **George Spillett** (57) (AL) is also still here. He is cousin to Frank at Court Lodge. His wife Harriett (59) is still with him, but his oldest children have left home. Edgar (19) and Frederic (sic)(15) both work as agricultural labourers. The family is also in a four-roomed cottage, but still find room for **Ivy Robson** (6) from Herne Bay, who is listed as a boarder. I suspect she is a foster child, taken in for a small remuneration.

The same sized cottage is occupied by **Edward Linkin** (30) (AL) and his wife Emma (26). They live with their children Annie (5), Arthur (4) and Margaret (1).

**George Pellett** (32) (AL) is from Ashford and has moved to the area with his wife Jane (29). Jane was born in Bridge and presumably knows the area well.

Our friend **Charles Vincer** (60) is next, with his wife Eliza (59) and his son Charles, who is now 20. Both men are agricultural labourers. Theirs was a reasonably comfortable existence in their little cottage, with two incomes, but there was no extra money for luxuries.

This pair almost certainly live in the house at 82 Shalmsford Street, known as Vincer Cottage.

**Richard Hoare** (86) still records his occupation as agricultural labourer. He lives with his wife Elizabeth (80) and they share their home with **Thomas Bartlett** (84) who boards with them. He also works as an agricultural labourer and was living on his own ten years ago. They are lucky enough to live in four rooms.

**George Hoare** (51) (AL) is Sarah's nephew and lives with his wife Louisa (nee Linkin) (50) and their daughter Alice Martha (9). Also in the house is their granddaughter Margarett (12), and this house has only three rooms I picture the girls sharing a bedroom. Alice is aunt to Margarett, who is the daughter of one of her older siblings.

George dies soon after the census and in 1895 Louisa marries William Sawkins. We can see them on the 1901 census living in Shalmsford Street with their blended family.

Another of Sarah's nephews, and cousin to George is **Jesse Hoare** (47) (AL) who is listed with his wife Jane (nee Pay) (43). This Jesse has five children at home, Jesse (18), Edward (16), Flora (8), Ernest (5) and May (2). Sons Jesse and Edward are both general labourers and the all live in a relatively large house. Jesse's son Harry now has his own household in the village.

One oddity on this record is the birthplace of Edward, which is recorded as being St Pancras, London. I wonder if Jane was visiting relatives during the last weeks of her pregnancy, or whether Edward has been adopted from another branch of the family. The couple married in 1882 and Edward does not appear on previous census returns.

Another of Sarah's sons, **Henry Hoare** (47) (AL) still lives with his wife Mary (44). We last saw them in 1871 when they lived on Bolts Hill. They live in a larger family than most as they have three wages coming in to the house. Their son William (17) works as a miller and Harry (14) is an agricultural labourer. The younger boys Thomas (11), Arthur (9) and Alfred (6) are still at school.

If the census return is to be taken literally, then **Edward Sladden** (45) (AL) lives in a house with more than five rooms. He lives with his wife Jane (43) and their son Edmond (14) who is also a farm labourer. They have one lodger, **Frederick Cork (**17) (AL), who has moved out of his home with his parents, Henry and Esther Cork, to live independently.

**Thomas Ballard** (41) (AL) appeared on the last census with his wife Jane (44). His household has changed a little since then; Jane's daughter from her previous marriage has now left and her mother has passed away. Daughters Eliza (12) and Florence (10) have been joined by Edith (5 months). Only Florence goes to school. Again, this family seem to live in a larger than average home.

farm labourer, and George (10) who goes to school.

We see **George Sims** (59) (AL) again on this census, who still lives with his wife Ann (59). Their daughters Alice, Mary and Clara have left home, but Ann (16) still lives with them and works in the paper mill.

An article in The Canterbury Journal and Farmers Gazette dated April 25th 1896 tells us that the family lived next door to Edward Mumford and his wife, although these two do not appear on this 1891 census.

Edward Mumford had apparently lost his job, taken to drinking and been struck with depression. The newspaper reports that he was brought before the petty sessions for attempting to commit suicide. Mrs Mumford had called George Sims at 6am as her husband was at the bottom of the garden, having slit his own throat. George helped Edward indoors and called the surgeon and the police. The surgeon was able to sew up the wound and Edward was taken to hospital, but not before IC Kemp, the policeman, had placed him under arrest him. Mrs Mumford told the court that her husband was good to her but 'drank very much'. Having further heard that he had now taken the pledge, the court dismissed charges.

As Edward is still with us on the 1901 census, I assume he stuck to the pledge and that his life, and that of his wife, improved.

**Richard Pay** (55) (AL) has boarded all his life, but is now seen in a household of his own, even though it is only two rooms. He is helped by a housekeeper, the widowed **Sophia Howshaw** (60) from Northamptonshire. She does not tick the 'employed' box, so I can surmise that perhaps there is more to this relationship than homeowner and housekeeper.

**Benjamin Elvy** (71) (AL) and his wife Betsey (68) were living with their son on the last census, but he has now moved out to start his own family. Benjamin was previously recorded as being a mariner, and I suppose that his agricultural work is undertaken on an ad hoc basis. Betsey works as a haberdasher.

The Baines family have managed to shoe-horn ten people into a cottage with only four rooms. **John Baines** (74) (AL) is the head of the household. His wife is Sarah (nee Martin) (42) was born in the Herne Workhouse married John in 1875. Their children are William (16) (AL), Eliza (14), Walter (10) and Thomas (8). The couple have also given a home to their niece **Nancy Prior** (7) and Sarah's mother **Caroline Marten** (66). Despite the large number of people in the house, they have still found room for a lodger, **James Dunks** (34) (AL) and also welcomed a guest, **Harry Smith** (18) (AL). Walter, James and Nancy go to school, but Eliza is now too old. She presumably helps her mother with the household chores and takes on odd work where she can find it. John and Sarah shared one room, and the other rooms allocated to males and females. The guest slept in the kitchen/living room or bunked in with the boys.

## Bolts Hill

Next in the street is **William Hall** (62) (AL) and his wife Elizabeth (60). William comes from Whitstable, and Elizabeth was born in nearby Blean. Their family has shrunk and their children Thomas (24) and Edward (18), who are both general labourers, are now the only two at home. The four-roomed, two-up-two-down house was ideal for the family with the parents in one bedroom and the boys (if I can still call them that) in the other.

**George Moat** (43) (AL) and his family continue to live in on Bolts Hill. His wife Mary (43) now has only eight children at home, as the oldest three have now left. The oldest daughter Mary (15) is listed as 'mother's help domestic'. The fact that the 'employed' box is not ticked suggests that she stays at home to help her own mother rather than working outside the home. The children that are still living at home are: John (16) (AL), Horace (11), Louisa (9), Clara (7), Jesse (4), Lily (2) and Alfred (5 months). Louisa, Clara and Jesse go to school, just down the road from them, and it must be a relief to Mary when they leave in the mornings; she will be pleased that they have a school so close to them; many children had to walk miles to get to school each day. She has one more child, in 1894, making a total of twelve. The fact that the number of rooms is not recorded for this household shows us that they had more than five.

A familiar face is that of **George Lyons** (46)(AL) who live in a dwelling of four rooms. These two households were recorded consecutively on the previous census, and this is reason to suppose they lived next door to each other. Like George Moat, George Lyons has a large family, which we have seen growing over the last twenty years. His wife Sarah (43) was born in Petham, but all the children were born in Chartham.

The oldest daughter recorded is Ellen (23) who is a glazier in the paper mill. She was not shown as being in the family home in 1881, so she may have been working away. Emily (13) is a mother's help/domestic, like her friend Mary Moat next door. Frederick (11), Alfred (9), William (7) and Charles (5) all go to school, while Kate (3) stays at home. She doubtless dotes on her older brothers and must look forward to the time when they come back at the end of the day. Albert and Mary Lyons have now left home.

## Trades and Professions

### Bolts Hill

Surprisingly, there is still roughly the same number of households living on Bolts Hill as were there ten years previously.

### Farmer George

First on the list are farmer **George Coltham** (87) at Court Lodge Farm and his housekeeper **Julia Stevens** (42), who we met previously. George is an employer not an employee, but there is no list of his employees now they do not live on site in tied cottages.

## Court Lodge Cottages

The family living at one of the cottages at Court Lodge is that of **Frank Spillett** (35), son of Thomas Spillett, who is a labourer in the paper mill. We have seen many Spilletts before, but this family is new to the Shalmsford Street hamlet, and I am confident that Frank is Thomas and Jemima's youngest child. Frank's wife Sarah (26) has three children under five to cope with, plus a new baby. She was born in Shepherdswell, but all the children were born in Chartham. **Jane Gambrell** (19) is visiting, and is no doubt here to help Sarah with the children, Frank (5), Allan (4), Ethel (2) and baby Ivy (3 months). She is taking time off from her work as a housemaid/domestic.

Next, **Sarah Spillett** (77) was born in Hastingleigh and is listed as the head of her household of one. She is Frank's mother, but likes to retain her independence, so is listed separately.

The next cottage is home to a couple without children. **William Hunt** (43) (AL) is husband to Frances (36). They have two boarders, **William A. Hazelwood** (17) (AL) and **William Williamson** (28) (AL).

Also in the cottages at Court Lodge is **Elizabeth Dixon** (82), a widower who now lives on her own. She occupies three rooms, which would be a bedroom, a parlour/living room and a kitchen/store room.

Next is **Henry Hart** (29), a young man with a growing family. He has moved to the area from Dunkirk, near Faversham. His wife Kate (25) comes from Hamstreet, but both children Gertrude (2) and Ethel (1) were born in Dunkirk like their father. Henry is a gardener, presumably at Court Lodge and it looks like he has taken over the work from the Stubberfields. Henry has four rooms in his cottage. This would be one parlour, one kitchen/living room, a bedroom for the parents and a bedroom for the children. This seems like an ideal situation while the children are young and there are only two of them.

The last family at Court Lodge Cottages is that of **James Jordan** (35), who is the farm bailiff. He supports his wife Rachel (35) and his six children. Rachel was born in Tenterden and all the children except the youngest child were born in Canterbury. The children are Alice (13), Walter (10), Charles (8), Mabel (6), Ellen (3) and James (1).

We read a sad report in the newspaper dated 14$^{th}$ February 1895. The country was in the grip of a severe frost and James almost froze to death while driving his employer home from Canterbury in a sleigh. He was pulled from his seat almost insensible and took several hours to regain full consciousness, he did eventually recover.

## A Gardener

Rose Cottage in home to **William H. Hayward** (49), who is a millwright. He lives with his wife Elizabeth (52), his daughter Elizabeth (25), a dressmaker, his son Henry (12) and his mother-in-law **Mary Wilson** (84). Elizabeth lists herself as neither employer nor employee, which suggests that she takes in needlework at home. The domestic sewing machine was in general use by this time, but it is likely that Elizabeth still used hand-sewing in the majority of her work; clothes would certainly have been hand-finished. Rose Cottage is on the south side of the railway line, immediately west of the level crossing and next to the Wesleyan Baptist church.

This house is mentioned by Selina Randolf in her book 'Chartham in Days of Old' when she is describing the old route of the main road from Shalmsford to Chartham. She describes how the road turned after the school, 'by Mr Hayward's house' towards Court Lodge and continued on what is now the other side of the railway line. The cottage is still there today and it has now been extended; it is listed on the 1911 census as having six rooms.

The Wesleyan Chapel

## Box Trees

This block of four-roomed cottages still houses six separate households, although they are later knocked into three and then one.

The first cottage is occupied by **William Stoner** (56). Originally from Slaugham, Sussex, who has served as village policeman for over a decade. His wife Martha (49) was born in Wonersh, Surrey. The children were all born in Chartham, Edith (12), Kezia (7) and Arthur (5). Their three older children had flown the nest. The family were previously living in Dover with their first child Grace, who died in 1874.

Another new face, is in the second cottage. **George Dray** (51) (AL), lives with his wife Caroline (40) and seven children. The oldest son Charles (15) works as an agricultural labourer, and the other children William (12), Julia (10), Caroline (9), Ernest (5) and Margaret (4) go to school. Only toddler John (1) is at home in the daytime. However, in the evenings and overnight it is exceptionally crowded in the little cottage. This is the time George no doubt escapes up the hill to 'The Cross Keys'.

Poor George seems to have been unlucky in life and in July 1897 the newspapers report that he was the victim of fraud. The con-man was sentenced to one month hard labour.

The third cottage is home to **Henry Samson** (29)(AL) who was born in Selling and lives with his wife Margaret (27) and son Henry (3). Margaret was born in Ospringe and Henry in Preston.

**William Sutton** (51) (AL) was born in Maidstone, but has now made his way to Chartham. He lives in the fourth cottage with his wife Eliza (48) is from Canterbury, and his son Harry (3) was born in Boughton.

Next is the family of **John Hulse** (22) a general labourer from Harbeldown and his wife Mary Jane (21). They have a new son, John (6 months old). I hope these two enjoy the quiet of their small household, as they have seven children by the turn of the century, and are joined by another five by 1911, making a total of 12.

Lastly in Box Trees Cottage are two familiar faces. **William Gibson** (63) (AL) is here with his wife Sarah (63). Sarah no longer works, but was previously listed as a laundress. The oldest son Jesse (34) is an agricultural labourer like his father. The couple have taken in a pair of lodgers, **Ellen and Alice Dibley**, who are both 13. They are not shown as attending school, but neither do they have an occupation. Both were born in Chartham. If the girls were being fostered, I would expect to see them listed as boarders, not lodgers. The girls are shown on the 1881 census with their parents, however there were ten children in the house, including two sets of twins, Ellen and

Alice (then aged 4) and their two-year-old brothers. On the 1911 census, it is shown that their mother had 15 children in total between 1865 and 1887. Perhaps their parents thought that the girls were old enough to fend for themselves, especially as they went together, and they paid the lodging fees.

## Box Trees House

Box Trees House is home to **Thomas Sutton** (37) a surgeon from Oxfordshire. He seems to share the house with **William Hulse** (33) a general labourer and his wife Jane (39). I can only assume that Jane works as a housekeeper as Thomas has no wife.

The footpath past Box Trees House which links Bolts Hill and Shalmsford Street is known locally as The Slip.

## Mount Pleasant

The house 'Mount Pleasant' has now been built. The name is taken from the local name for the hillside on which it stands, and has now been shortened to 'The Mount'. It is home to **Philip Platten** (56) who is the schoolmaster, and has moved her from Box Tree Cottages. In March 1890 he is listed as a ruling councillor in The Primrose League, which can be broadly described as a society promoting working-class conservatism. It was a hugely successful movement in its day, credited with nurturing the young Winston Churchill.

Philip and his whole family were born in Norfolk, but his wife has recently died. He now lives with his daughter Gertie (22) and his niece Ella (25). The family are looked after by domestic servant **Emma Barnes** (23).

## An Independent Woman

Firstly, **Ann Newington** (86) is now the head of her household, as her husband has passed away. She is 'living on her own means' which indicates that she has a pension or savings. Her daughter Amelia (64) is still in the house, and she has now reverted to her maiden name (she was previously Rudduck). Amelia's children have moved out and Ann has taken in a boarder, **William Wagstaff** (22) who teaches at the school. He was born in Blockley in Worcestershire, so has travelled a long way in search of an appointment. As a boarder rather than a lodger, he ate his meals with the family as this was included with the rent.

## Working at the Asylum

**Albert Dale** (35) has a job at the St Augustine's Asylum. His job title is 'lunatic attendant' and he has moved here from Elham. His wife Rosina (36) is from London and works as both a seamstress and paper sorter, which indicates to me that she takes in sewing work on a piece work basis, which she undertakes after her work at the paper mill in Chartham, either making basic garment pieces before they are sent to be made up elsewhere or producing simple undergarments.

Their granddaughter **Elizabeth Adams** (12) lives with them, and takes the strain of running the household away from Rosina, who works such long hours.

## A Paper Mill Employee

Lastly on Bolts Hill is **Charles Richardson** (42) from Dover who has moved here to work in the paper mill where he is a paper maker. His wife Susan (31) is a self-employed tailoress from Suffolk. They have no children, but have adopted **Hilda Fagg** (5) who was born in London, who is presumably related in some way to the local Fagg family. **Carrie Ring** aged 3 is noted as being a visitor to the house. As their family is small, they have been able to take in two boarders, **Georgina Lother** (25) from London and **Lizzie Clifton** (21) from Gainsborough. Both are Salvation Army officers and worshipps and works at hall which once stood at the junction of Bolts Hill and Shalmsford Street having on 13th June 1889. In a four-room house, this number of people was a tight fit. Charles and Susan had one room and Georgina and Lizzie shared the other. The two girls may have gone in with the adults or curled up on a settle in the nice warm kitchen – not too bad an option!

## 'The Cross Keys'

Next is 'The Cross Keys' pub, with **Henry Swaffer** (41) as the publican. He is from Great Chart, and his wife Eliza (28) is from London. His daughter Bessie (5) was also born in Great Chart, so Eliza could have been working there when they met. They have moved here from Ashford.

## A Baker

**Walter West** (41), a baker, lives with his wife Jane (40), his niece **Nellie Payne** (15) and his nephew **John Cooper** (24). John works as a butcher and the family live in Myrtle Cottage which are now numbers 123-127 Shalmsford Street.  Both men are employed by other people. It is noted that Walter comes from Farnham and that Jane was born on the Isle of Sheppey

**Thomas Barham** (53) lives in Myrtle Cottages with his daughter Charlotte (26). Thomas works as a carpenter and Charlotte is a dressmaker, reproducing fashionable dresses from fashion books and commercial patterns as well as from her own observations of the fine ladies in Canterbury.

## Two Carpenters

One of the three cottages known as Myrtle Cottages is occupied by **William Ruck** (52), who is also a carpenter. He still lives with his wife Maria (55) and their children Lavinia (24), Benjamin (21), Maud (15) and Fred (13). Their older son William has moved across the road with his new family.

**Benjamin Pay** (43) the carpenter is the next to be recorded in Shalmsford Street. His house is larger than five rooms and holds himself, his wife Elizabeth (40) and his seven children. All children were born in Chartham. The oldest three work: Benjamin (16) is a yard boy, James (14) is a garden boy and Walter (13) is a teacher at the Board School. Norris (10), Hilda (8) and Elizabeth (5) go to school and Mary (3) is the only one left at home during the day. Mary Ann has left home. Norris will die before the next census, passing away in 1897.1881

The cottage on the corner of Bobbin Lodge Hill is known locally as Pay's Cottage, and it is likely to be this home.

## A Wheelwrigh

The next household in that of **William Bangham** (44) the wheelwright and his wife Mary (40), who is from Bobbing, near Sittingbourne. They live in a four-roomed house with their daughter Clara (12), who must be delighted to have her own room when she sees how many siblings her friends have to share with.

## Paper Mill Employees

**Elizabeth (Betsey) Vincer** (44) is now a duster in the paper mill. She lives with her

Myrtle Cottages,

daughter Frances (16) who works in the paper mill as well, as a rag cutter. Carrie Vincer (3) is listed as Elizabeth's cousin and is from Pimlico in London. The three women must be quite comfortable in their three rooms, with two incomes.

A duster worked with the newly-cut rags that were being processed for use in paper-making. Once sorted and cut, the rags were processed in a large rotating machine to remove small particles and dust.

**Thomas Saker** (25) from Blean is new to the area. Like Charles Richardson, he has moved to the area to work as a paper maker at the mill. His wife Sarah (nee Peet) (21) was born in Chartham, as were their children George (3) and Frederick (2). The family live in three rooms.

**George Cook** works at the paper mill as a paper maker. He lives with his wife Susanna (37) and four children; Albert (10), Ellen (8), and Amy (6) are all at school, while George is now 13 and old enough to work, so he has found employment as a grocer's assistant. Again, they have four rooms.

## General Labourers

**James Cullen** (23) was last seen training as an apprentice to George Kingsland. He now works as a general labourer, so it is possible he did not manage to complete his training as a blacksmith. He now lives with his wife Emily (23) from Molash and his new son Frederick (10 months). They have three rooms in their house.

**Henry Wright** (46) also has a large family crammed into four rooms. He moved here from Molash to marry local girl Eliza Vincer (44). Curiously, Henry is also noted as being crippled from birth, but he still works as a farm labourer. Their children are Mary (22), Eliza (18), Caroline (15), Henry (13) and Thomas (6). We last saw this family living in Box Tree Cottages, but they have now moved to Shalmsford Street. Henry's age has been recorded in error, either on the previous census or on this one, as he has not aged at all over the past decade. Henry works as a farm labourer, and Eliza's mother **Esther Vincer** is listed as a boarder. She is listed as being single, for as we know she was a single mother to Eliza on previous census returns.

In researching this little family, I found another strange anomaly. By looking at Mary's wedding certificate from 1899, I found that she was recorded as Mary Vincer (not Mary Wright), which was odd. I then realised that Mary was born before Henry and Eliza had married, thus taking her mother's surname. Even though she lived with Henry, it looks like she never officially took his name, so Vincer was the name she needed to use on the marriage certificate.

**Henry Amos** (69) is still working as a general labourer and now lives with **Harriet Wickenden** (54) who is his housekeeper. Harriet has moved here from Hastings. Both are widowed.

Listed next is **Henry Cook** (62) and his wife Charlotte (59). Daughter Lydia has left, but son Arthur (17) is still at home. They have taken in a lodger, who is an engine fitter. **John Crowther** (33) comes from Richmond in Surrey. Henry still works as a farm labourer and Arthur is a grocer's assistant. I wonder how they all fitted into a house with only four rooms. John either shares a room with Arthur or has been given the front room as his own private space.

**Albert Gibson** is another new face, and again lives in four rooms. His wife Eliza (34) is from West Malling and his son George (4) was born in Birchington. The new baby, Frank (2 months) was born in Chartham. Albert works as a general labourer.

**Henry Hayward** (40) seems to be new to the Shalmsford Street area. He works as a paper finished and supports a large household. However, the family have four incomes coming in plus the money they earn from a lodger. For this reason, they live in a house that is larger than five rooms. Henry's wife Mary (38) has no occupation, but their oldest two boys work. Harry (16) is a paper finisher like his father, and Frederick (14) is a paper machine boy. The next three children, Frank (11), Annie (9), Lilian (7) and Gertrude (4) all go to school, while Ernest (2) and Leonard (3 months) stay at home. With eight children plus a husband to feed and clothe, Mary will be grateful for the help of her mother-in-law **Annie Cook** (70). Henry's father Thomas (66) also lives with them, and works as a stoker and engine driver. The house is large enough to accommodate a lodger, **Florence Miller** (18) who earns her living as a pupil teacher at the school.

**Thomas Newton** (43) is another familiar face, who now has two more children in his family. He works as a general labourer while his wife Jane (40) stays at home. He oldest son Frederick (18) is now an apprentice to an engine maker, but lives at home, rather than living with his employer. Henry (10) and Alice (7) go to school while Thomas (3) stays home with his mother.

**Charles Webb** (39) a general labourer from Reading has married local girl Cecilia (37) and they live with their seven children in four rooms. The oldest son, Charles (16) is out at work as a baker's assistant all day, while William (10) and Joseph (8) go to school. Harriet (12) along with younger brothers Alfred (5), Thomas (3) and Ernest (1) are at home, either helping or getting in the way. No doubt Cecilia sends the boys out as often as she can, while Harriet, who has been crippled since birth, helps with sedentary tasks like preparing vegetables and entertaining her brothers.

## An Engineer and Farmer

**Thomas Rodwell** (36) is an engineer and farmer, and he notes that he is an employer, there is no record of how many men he employs. He has moved here from Watford, and his wife Ann (41) is from Loose in Kent. Their children Herbert (10), Frank (9), Edith (6) go to school and Bertha (3) stays home.

## The Grocer

**James Nash** (44) is the village grocer and is listed as an employer. He lives with his wife Elizabeth (41) and their two children. His daughter Jessie is 22 and his son Percy is just one month old. James has taken on an apprentice, **Frederick Penny** who lives in the house with them while he learns his trade, and they also have one servant, **Elizabeth Butterfield** (14) from Clapham. **Mercy Gipson** (69) is visiting the family on the night of the census. Luckily, they occupy one of the larger houses in Shalmsford Street.

## Farm Labourers

**George Harlow** (53) works as a farm labourer and supports a family of seven. As he is on a low wage, he can only afford a three-roomed house but still loves to have his family around him. His wife Caroline (41) was born in Wye and the children were born in very different parts of the county. Lizzie (18) was born in Eastbourne, Margaret (13) was born in High Minnis, Kent, Kate (11) was born in Woodchurch, Kent, and Frederick (7) was born in Faversham. George's grandson Percy (3) was born in Crundale and also lives with them; his mother was George's daughter Annie. Kate and Frederick go to school.

**Robert Fearn** (31) is a farm labourer living with his wife Eliza (46) in a four-roomed cottage. He is surrounded by women, as his daughter Ida (3) lives with them as well as Emily Barker (15) and Florence Barker (6) who are both listed as daughters-in-law. However, further research shows that Robert and Eliza have only been married four years, and Emily and Florence are Eliza's children from a previous relationship and are in fact Robert's step-daughters.

I wonder if they live in one of the four cottages now known as Fern Cottages, now two semi-detached dwellings at 81-83 Shalmsford Street.

**Edward Link** (47) still works as a farm labourer and lives with his wife Lydia (51). He squeezes his family into three rooms, which was a tight fit at night, although they were out at work during the day. Louisa (17) works as a glazier in the paper mill, William (13) is a farm labourer. The younger sons Sidney (11) and Henry (8) are at school. Edward's step-son Charles has now left home.

The next recorded household is also full to overflowing. **William Cork** (40) works as a farm labourer to support his wife Emma (41) and their four children, Harry (14), William (11), Stephen (7) and Albert (3). They also have **Ellen Smith** (21) living with them, who is shown as being their daughter-in-law. However, if she had married their son, she would have taken his name, so this remains a mystery.

## The Coal Merchant

**Charles Pettit** (30) is a coal merchant and lives in a larger house than many, having more than five rooms. He lives with his wife Elizabeth (28) and their three children. Only Charles comes from outside the village, having been born in East Farleigh. The children are John (7), Sidney (5) and Charles (2). The two older boys are in school. Charles' brother lodges with Sarah Hoare nearby.

## A Coal Carter

**Henry Cork** (43) is now a coal carter. He lives with his wife Esther (45) who was born in Linstead. They have two sons still at home, Alfred (13) and Percy (8). For a small family in a small house (4 rooms) it seems odd that they would keep a housekeeper, **Mary March** (21), but it could be that Esther is ill or is nursing Henry and cannot manage the housework herself. Three of their children have now left the home. Frederick is now lodging with the Sladdens. Alfred is only 13 and already works as a farm labourer. Their cottage has four rooms, which was divided into three bedrooms (boys sharing) and one kitchen/living room.

Henry dies in 1893 aged 46 and is buried on 18th November

A Captain in the Salvation Army

The Salvation Army Hall

William Jarvis (48) works as a general labourer and lives with his wife Fanny (47) and his family in one of the typical four-roomed cottages in the street. His daughter Matilda (24) is a Salvation Army captain and is recorded as a preacher on the census return. William's next daughter Annie (13) is no longer at school, but no occupation is recorded. The next child, William (10) is shown as suffering from epileptic fits, severe enough for the enumerator to feel it was necessary to record it as a disability. Perhaps Annie stays at home to help lo

after him. The two younger children Ida (7) and Harry (5) both go to school. Apart

from William, the whole family was born in Chilham.

The Salvation Army had a strong presence in Shalmsford, providing not only a place of worship and relief of hardship, but also 'treat' days for workers and children. On several occasions, the school was closed because excursions to such places as Margate. Originally called The Christian Mission, The Salvation Army was started by William Booth.

## A Water Bailiff

Sarah's son William Hoare (35) works as a water bailiff to support his wife and children, all of whom were born in Chartham. William's job is to maintain the fishing rights on the river and is a kind of customs official. His wife Emma (35) stays at home with Mabel (3) while Robert (11) and Frances (8) are at school.

## A Coalman

**George Gipson** (26) seems to live a happy life. He is a carter, working for the coal merchant at the yard which lay next to the Salvation Army Hall, and lives with his wife Ellen (nee Hulse) (27) in their little two-up-two-down cottage. The second bedroom is occupied by their sons George (6) and William (4) who are at school all day, and little Sidney (1) stays with his mother in the day and may well still be in with his parents at night.

## Two Landladies

Richard's sister-in-law **Sarah Hoare** (72) lives on her own now her sons have moved away, and makes ends meet by taking in lodgers. She currently has two: **Frank Pettit** (26) and his wife Matilda (nee Moat)(20). Frank is a general labourer and was born in East Farleigh. Matilda was born in Chartham and married Frank in 1888. Ten years ago she was living with her family on Bolts Hill. Richard's brother George is still alive, and is living in Shalmsford Street with his daughter Harriet.

We saw **Sarah Burchett** on the last census living with her widowed brother. I do not know what kind of house they lived in previously, but she is now in a four-roomed cottage. She does not give an occupation, but it is clear from the census that her incuome comes in the form of rent from her lodgers. Three people lodge in the house, **Alfred Boughton** (28) (AL), **Thomas Webb** (52)

(AL) and **Jesse Austen** (69) (AL). I assume that Sarah keeps one bedroom and the others are grateful for the use on one shared room between them plus the use of the kitchen facilities.

## A Blacksmith

**William Rose** (33) has moved here from Fordingbridge in Hampshire to take up a job as blacksmith. He lives with his wife Lucy (32) and their sons Henry (8) and William (5). Henry goes to school, but for some reason William does not. They have only three rooms in their house.

## Five Bricklayers

**Harry Hoare** (27), son of Jesse, who works as a bricklayer's labourer and lives in a four-roomed house. His wife Elizabeth (25) is from Bristol and has her hands full with Edith (2) and Arthur (6 months).

**James Vidgen** (39) the bricklayer is still here in Shalmsford Street, with his ever-expanding family. He and his wife Emily (39) now have four children at home, William (13), Ethel (10) and Arthur (4) who are at school, plus Edith (2). They have also given a home to Emily's unmarried sister **Jane Hoare** (40). I wonder how they arranged the sleeping arrangements with only four rooms in the house. I suspect the girls slept in with their Aunt Jane while the boys were separate. James is a bricklayer, and is an employee. Jane and Emily are both daughters to Sarah Hoare, who still lives in the village, although their father John has passed away.

**James Tritton Adams** (65) still lives with just his wife Rebecca (64). He still works as a bricklayer, although maybe in a more supervisory role than when he was younger. Rebecca will be keen to keep in touch with her children and hear news of new arrivals.

We have watched this family grow through the whole of the Victorian era, and it is now sad to say goodbye to some of them. Rebecca dies in July 1893 aged 67.

**William Ruck** (30) is now qualified as a journeyman bricklayer, which was a long apprenticeship, but well worth it. He lives with his wife Elizabeth (30) and his new son Fred (3 months). Their four-roomed house will no doubt fill with children over the coming years, and Elizabeth can call on her mother-in-law Maria, who lives opposite, to help at any time.

Based on the information to hand, I guess that the Banghams and the Rucks live in the two semi-detached cottages now known as 84-86 Shalmsford Street.

**Henry Cork** (68) is in an even more overcrowded house, having only three rooms and three adult sons living with him. He and his wife Jane (64) will be comfortably off as Henry works as a bricklayer. Their sons Edward (27) and Jesse (19) work as bricklayers labourers and Charles (22) is a gardener. As they will be working long hours they are presumably more than happy to come home to their Mum's cooking and to share a room at night. However, by the time of the next census in 1901, both Charles and Jesse have their own homes.

Henry dies in February, aged 70, and is buried in Chartham.

## A River Keeper

**James M. Hoare** (52) is yet another cousin, and is still with us; he now works as a river keeper. He lives with his wife Emma (51). His two daughters bring in a wage, with Elizabeth (20) being a dressmaker and Ellen (14) working as a domestic servant. Also living with them is Rhoda Hoare (4) who is listed as James' granddaughter. Her father is George Hoare, but as far as I can find out, his father is Joseph, so I cannot see how she is related to James. They fit neatly into their house with four rooms, with the parents taking one bedroom and the girls in the other.

Further investigation of this fascinating family tells us that James returned to the USA with his family and lived there until his death in 1904. His grave is in Syracuse, New York, and adds some more details to the information we already have about this family.

James' wife Emma died in New York in 1897, but he is survived by his sons Alfred and Frederick and by four daughters, who are now all married. Ann has married Henry Spillett, Fannie has married Ezekial Warden, Elizabeth is now Mrs Percival, and Ellen (known as Nellie) is now Mrs Stephen Spillett. The whole family live in New York.

Stephen and Henry Spillett are brothers, and are the sons of Henry (Harry) and Charlotte Spillett, who met while working as servants at Burnt House Farm in Chartham. They also moved to New York with their sons Henry, Stephen and George and their daughter Emily and lived there until their deaths.

## A Chimney Sweep

**John Horace Gibson** (30) is a chimney sweep, who works for himself. He supports his wife Susan (32) and son John Horace (6) by taking in lodgers. **William Boughton** (61), a bricklayer, and **Henry Spillett** (73) a farm servant, lodge with them. Henry was the man shown as the husband of Phoebe on previous census returns. Both men are widowers, and manage to squeeze into four rooms with the family. Luckily for young John, he is out at school all day.

## An Asylum Worker

**James Newton** (38) works as a water purifier at the asylum. He lives in four rooms with his wife Mary (31), three sons and two daughters. His son James (12) is a shepherd boy, while Walter (11), Eva (8) and Montague (6) go to school. Only Harriet (3) is at home and Edward (4) go to school, while Sidney (2) is at home

## A Life Insurance Salesman

John Noble (34) in another four-roomed cottage is a newcomer. He works as a life assurance agent and was born in Canterbury. His wife Jane (33) is from Bonnington. The oldest boys Horace (10).

## A Miller

Yet another new face is **John Gore** (26) from Littlebourne, just to the east of Canterbury. He is employed as a miller, presumably at the Corn Mill on Canterbury Road. His wife Maria (30) is from Kilndown, and their daughter Edith (2) was born in Chartham. They have one boarder, **Percy Miles** (18) from Hoathe, who works as a butcher.

The Primitive Methodist Church

## A Builder

**John Wood** (47) is still in Shalmsford Street working as a builder with his wife Annie (51). Emma **Mumford**, is recorded as their daughter-in-law, but was previously listed as John's step-daughter. John's age has incorrectly been recorded as 47 when it should be 67. John is an employer, who had an impressive team working for him in the 1881 census, but this information is now unrecorded. This house is larger than five rooms.

## A New Baker and Grocer

**Joseph Watson** (32) and his wife Mary (32) work hard to make a living. Joseph is a baker and grocer, and Mary is proud to be listed as his assistant. They have a house with more than five rooms for themselves and their family, plus two live-in servants. Their children Eleanor (8) and Mary (6) go to school while Ernest (3) is watched by his mother while she helps in the shop. The servants are **Samuel Harlow** (21), who we last saw living with his family, who is now a journeyman baker and **Jane Harlow** (16) who works as a general servant. Jane is the daughter of John and Charlotte Harlow while Sam is the son of Samuel and Ann.

I think that this family must have taken over the shop from Phineas Shrubsole, living in what is now The Old Bakery.

It is interesting to read on the website of The Primitive Methodist Church that Joseph Watson was instrumental in setting up the church in Shalmsford Street. I can only surmise that it is the same Joseph Watson recorded on the census.

*One of the most wonderful revivals witnessed in Kent laid the foundations of our Shalmsford Street society. The revival began in 1885, and continued for ten years. The whole neighbourhood was moved, and numbers were converted. Mr. Joseph Watson, the leader of our work here, has been a most acceptable local preacher for thirty-seven years. For fourteen years he was on the local school board, acting for three years as chairman, with the rector as vice-chairman. His sturdy Nonconformity, and growing Christian influence, has done much to give our church a standing, and to render it successful amidst strong Anglican influences.*

*Christian Messenger 1914/301*

## A Horseman

**William Taylor** (63) (AL) was born in Chartham, but his wife Emily (37) was born in Wateringbury, near Maidstone. They have one son, Ernest (5), and live in three rooms.

William is later recorded as a 'horseman', and I assume he worked with horses all his life, building up an impressive set of skills.

The job of the horseman was a skilled one, encompassing the roles of animal handler, vetinary practitioner, farrier, and leather-worker. He was required at his work hours before the others in order to feed and prepare the horses for the day's work, and then lead them through an eight-hour day before bringing them in, feeding and settling them for the night, attending to any sickness or injury and maintaining the harnesses. He was recognisable in his trademark whipcord breeches.

Horses were used for a variety of farm and field work, including pulling a plough and hauling cut timber from the woods.

## The Butcher

**Alfred Hudson** (33) is the butcher and also lives in a large house. He is listed as being an employer. He supports his wife Elizabeth (25) and their son Herbert (2).

## Two Shepherds

The house of **John Daniels** (44) is very overcrowded. He lives in four rooms with his wife Clara (37) and their seven children. He was recorded on the last census as a milkman and gardener, but has now changed jobs. As a shepherd, he will often be out of the house for days at a time, and often overnight in lambing season. Their son Joseph (14) works as a farm yard boy, but Mary (12), Frank (11), Edwin (9) and Richard (7) still go to school. Youngsters Arthur (2) and Ernest (1) are at home during the day.

We see **William Rumley** (25) lives in Shalmsford Bridge Cottages, now numbers 1-5 Shalmsford Street, with his wife Flora (21). Previously he was living with his family. This cottage has more than five rooms, as does William Bushell's. William works as a shepherd, and the couple have three sons in the village before moving to Faversham, where William becomes a cemetery curator.

## Two Engine Drivers

The household of **John Hulse** (55) the engine driver will be much calmer. He also lives in four rooms, but has only two children. He and his wife Charlotte (51) now have two sons, Harry (13), who works as a farm labourer, and George (10) who goes to school.

**William Bartlett** (52) is an engine driver living in a larger house than many of his neighbours. He lies with his wife Sophy (42), their daughter Sophy (12) and another daughter May (10 months). We saw the family on the last census living with Sophy's parents. They must be glad to have their own house now.

## The Farm Bailiff

**Stephen Hopkins** (54) and his family are new to the street. He lives at Shalmsford Farm where he is employed as the farm bailiff. His family consist of wife Emily (52) and their three daughters Frances (8), Amy (6) and Daisey (sic)(4).

It was sad for me to find The Canterbury Journal and Farmers Gazette dated 24th Dec 1898, a report recounting the death of Stephen's son, found dead in his pram after a fit.

## The Publican at 'The George'

'The George' pub is still owned and run by publican **James Stupples** (54). James wife is not recorded on the census, and he lives only with his son Leon (25) who works as a groom, and daughter Rose who no doubt keeps house in the absence of her mother with the help of her sister Minnie (15). Maud (9) is still at school. They family have one boarder, **Sidney Gambrill** (24) who is also a farm bailiff, and presumably works over the road with Stephen Hopkins. Sidney was 19 when we saw him at home with his parents, so he seems to have 'lost' five years. Perhaps he feels a need to keep up with Leon.

A mention of 'The George' appears in the October 2nd edition of The Thanet Advertiser in 1897.

The newspaper reports upon the unfortunate accident of a man from Thanet who was driving an overloaded van of furniture from Ramsgate to Ashford. He handed the reins to another man while he stood up to put on his coat, missed his footing and fell from the vehicle. He hit his head and died soon afterwards in hospital. George Jesse Harlow, who had been in 'The George', gave evidence at the inquest that they had found the man unconscious and sent for the doctor and that his companion had been sober at the time of the accident. It was ruled as death by misadventure. Reading between the lines, George's report that he 'proceeded along the road with others' may give the impression of a more sedate exit from the pub than actually happened.

The pub continues to be the centre of village life, and appears regularly in the papers, with some news being of a more savoury kind than others.

The local paper reported that the annual carnival organised by The Carnival Society started from 'The George', as usual. Apart from the date of 14th November, it does not give any further details. Carnivals in rural communities were held during slack periods when work was scarce, whereas carnivals in seaside areas were held in the summer to attract tourists.

In 1895, the newspaper again reports on the carnival, stating that there were 50 people involved, as well as a band. Messrs Hall and Hoare were to be thanked for organising it.

Another incident at 'The George', reported in in September 1890 tells us that it was a favourite pub with the itinerant hop pickers. The newspaper reports on a fight outside the pub involving up to 100 men. Hand-picking continued up until the 1960s, when mechanisation finally took over.

## An Independent Woman

The widow **Harriet Stupperfield** (77) lives on her own means with her daughter Mary (43) who does not work. They money they do have enables them to live in a house with more than five rooms.

## A Single Mother?

**Francis Fagg** (22) and her son Charles (8 months) have four rooms in their home. She does not give an occupation, so I assume her husband is away from home for the one night only. She was born in Monks Horton in Kent, and her son was born in Elmstead.

## Working on the Railway

**George Epps** (63) and his wife Maria (67) are now enjoying the space in their cottage which is the standard four-roomed size, or they may be missing their granddaughter Emily Fraser who was staying with them at the time of the last census. George works as a plate-layer on the L.C.D. Railway (The London, Chatham and Dover Rail Line), and as this line does not pass through Chartham, he will be getting up early to travel by train to Canterbury and then to his place of work.

## Three Wheelwrights

**George Vant** (56) is new to Shalmsford Street, and he works as a wheelwright. He comes from Westwell, and his wife Charlotte (48) comes from Selling.

**William Cruttenden** (69) a wheelwright from Milton has moved into Shalmsford Street and employs men under him. He lives with his wife Ann (54) who was born in Christchurch in Hampshire. The fact that there is work for three wheelwrights, who may or may not work together, shows the continued importance of wooden farm equipment in the area.

William's son **Robert Cruttenden** (37), also a wheelwright, now has two more children. He lives with his wife Mary (33) and his three children William (11), Arthur (8) and Winifred (3) in a house with more than five rooms. In 1888 we find an advert from Cruttenden and Son offering for sale a 2-horse iron hop shim. William will be 18 by this time, and will have joined his father in the business.

## Working with Wood

**Henry Spillett** (60) still works as a woodreeve and lives with his wife Sophia (59). With so many of their family still in the village, they are not lonely in their later years, and are their nephews Frank and George are regular visitors.

## A Travelling Shoemaker

**Frederick Thorrington** (49) is a cordwainer (shoemaker). He lives with his daughter Louisa Thorrington (17) and his son-in-law **James Halls** (20), who is also a cordwainer. James is shown as an employer, so I assume he employs Frederick. A side-note tells us that

Frederick has been lame since birth, so his occupation, which involves minimal moving around is ideal. They are lucky enough to live in a four-roomed house.

Interestingly, Louisa was born in Plumstead in Kent, but both men come from Essex. Frederick was born in Messing and James in Great Wakering. Louisa later marries Frederick Cork and moves to Faversham, so is not married to James. 'Son-in-law' is often a synonym for adopted son, which is further borne out by the fact that he is listed as being single.

## A Carpenter

**John Gipson** (52) and his family were all born in Chartham and now live at 51 Park View, next to the Primitive Methodist Chapel. John works as a rough carpenter, and his wife Harriet (nee Hoare) (54) looks after the house, including her father, **George Hoare,** who is now 88. John's son James (13) now works as a farm labourer and his adopted son George (20) (his nephew) also lives with them while he works at the mill as a paper maker. Harriet has a tough time ahead of her as both her husband and her father die before the next census is taken. John's occupation is recorded on his death certificate as 'hurdle-maker'.

It is sad to note on the 1911 census that Harriett discloses that she has given birth to 14 children, only five of whom have survived. John and Harriet were married in 1855, and their first child arrived a year afterwards, followed by four children who lived to adulthood and four babies who were baptised but died in infancy. The last child who lived was James, born in 1877, so somewhere amongst these were four more children who were stillborn or died in very early infancy. Harriett was lucky to survive.

## A Railway Man

**Joseph Oliver** (64) is a platelayer on the railway. He lives with his wife Elizabeth (55) and their son Charles (16), who works as a blacksmith's labourer. Also in the house is Edmond Oliver (11), the couple's grandson.

## A Retired Man

**Alfred Foreman** (65) is still with us, but his household has changed, somewhat. We have followed Alfred since he moved to the area 30 years ago. He was once a builder and is now a glazier employing other men. In Chartham terms, that is usually a jargon term for a specific job at the paper mill, but as Alfred was once a builder, I wonder if, in this case, he is a glazier in the modern way, ie putting in windows. This is an affluent household, with almost all the occupants bringing in a wage. Alfred's children have left home, but his niece and two nephews have now moved in. **Agnes Miles** (23) is his niece, and she works as a companion. The first nephew is **William Oliver** (34), who works as a tailor, and the second is **George Oliver** (15) who currently works as a domestic servant. Alfred employs two servants**, Jane Shilling** (30) and **John Souten** (24). He also gives a home to apprentice **George Fon** (18). Nobody in this household was born in the area.

We continue to read about Alfred in the local newspaper. 1891 was the year of The Great Gale and the Canterbury Journal and Farmer's Gazette of November 14th 1891 records how Alfred rescues a girl from a fallen tree. Mr Foreman was walking in St Peter's Street, Canterbury when he heard screams and ran to help. A large branch had fallen onto two children; Alfred rescued one, and another man rescued the other.

I have also found evidence that he was active in other areas of the community.

A plaque was installed in Hernhill church after Alfred's death in 1909. It reads:
IN MEMORIAM
Alfred Foreman of Chartham
Formerly of this parish
He was a member of Canterbury Cathedral Voluntary choir and also a member of the Band of change ringers.
He assisted in ringing the old year out
And the new year in at the Cathedral
For 50 years in succession.

## Two Widows

**Elizabeth Homersham** (77) lives on her own means with her daughter **Mary Philpott** (42), and **Mary Speed** (68) a nurse. I assume that Mary Speed nurses Elizabeth as she is not listed as either a lodger or a boarder. **William Moore** (76) is a retired farmer, and is listed as a boarder. Elizabeth dies in Seasalter in November of this year.

**Eliza Pay** (68) works as a laundress and lives on her own.

## No Occupation Given

**John Young**, whose fortunes we have followed for many years, still lives on his own. He is now recorded as being 77 years old, so he seems to have gained an extra sixteen years in the last decade! He lives in a cottage with three rooms.

## A Charwoman

**Ann Fisher** (61), now a widow, is head of her household, which has three wages coming in. We saw Ann and her husband on the 1871 census, but William died in 1885. Ann works as a charwoman, and her sons Frederick (25) and Edward (24) are a bricklayer's labourer and a general labourer respectively. Ann, you will remember, was the son of James and Jane Link.

## A Policeman

The next cottage, of a similar size, is occupied by **Stephen Stone** (51), a police constable. He does not have a wife so his daughter Elizabeth (15) acts as housekeeper. He has two sons, Stephen (13) who is already out at work as a bird boy, in the fields all day scaring birds from the crops, and Albert (11) who is still at school.

1895 was a very hard winter and we read in the newspaper that Mr Stone is now an ex-policeman and was found by Alfred Foreman almost frozen to death, leaning against a hedge. He was taken home and luckily suffered no lasting ill effects, although it took several hours to bring his back to full sensibility.

## Two Laundresses

**William Bushell** (69) (AL) lives with his wife Hannah (69) and granddaughter Elizabeth Law (15) in Shalmsford Bridge Cottages. Both women work as laundresses.

## A Bootmaker

Next is a property that is listed as being in Shalmsford Lane, which is a road that either no longer exists or has been renamed Thruxted Lane. It is the home of **Ambrose Burchett** (38) now a self-employed bootmaker and his family. It is interesting that he calls himself a bootmaker, not a shoemaker. Perhaps this is his speciality? We met this family when they were newly-weds living with Ambrose' father George. Ambrose and his wife Alice (31) now have three children, Arthur (10), William (8) and Ethel (3). This is a large house with more than five rooms.

Railway Crossing Cottage

## A Crossing Attendant

We come next to the address given as Railway Crossing, which was the crossing by on Thruxted Lane. A very close inspection of the 1907 tithe map shows a very small cottage right by the crossing, which has now been demolished, but which was similar if not identical to Riverside Gatehouse in Riverside, Chartham.

It is home to **James Stacey** (50) who is a platelayer on the railway. He lives with his wife Mary (60), his son James (24) who works as a labourer at the paper mill and James' wife Margaret (22). James and Margaret have two daughters, Margaret (2) and Arbin (6 months). James and Mary's daughters have now moved out. Mary gives her occupation as Railway Gate Keeper. This house has four rooms. Sadly, Arbin Dulcibella later dies, aged 8.

James lived in a four-roomed cottage by the crossing on Thruxted Lane. His home was in a similar style to the Riverside Gatehouse still in existence in Chartham, if not identical. The carved barge boards under the eaves play into the architect's dream of a Romantic rural England, as did the cement dressings around the doors and windows, playfully giving the cottage charm if not practicality. The solid nine-inch walls were enough to keep out the elements and some of the noise from the passing trains. The house was built when the railway was first introduced, circa 1850.

This couple are very fortunate to both have jobs with the railway, as railway workers earn almost twice as much as labourers. Mary could attend to her household duties while waiting for the next train to arrive – a perfect arrangement for childcare.

## A Needlewoman

We met **Mary Rumley** (63) in the last census, with a house full of boys. She still has a large family around her, but some faces have changed. Now all the boys are working, she herself has given up work. Mary's daughter Elizabeth (31) has returned home and supports herself by taking in needlework, specialising in shirts. William has left home, but the four boys, George (29), Alfred (27), who has come back home, Charles (23) and Edward (21), all work as farm labourers. The family has four rooms, so the boys would share one bedroom while Mary and Elizabeth share the other. Mary lives not too far away from her son William.

## A Gardener

Also at this end of the village, we have John Link (57) who is employed as a gardener and lives at Branch Cottage with his wife Ann (74). Their daughter Emily Element (29) is on a visit from London with her three children Edith (7), Daisy (6) and Hilda (4). This house is in the Shalmsford Street Hamlet as previously defined for this study. He is brother to Edward Link

## A Nurse

Widow Maria **Mumford (50) is shown as being a** nurse. She is head of her household, living with her children Rosa (24), David (13) (AL) and Violet (12). They have four rooms in their home at Shalmsford Bridge Cottages. The Salvation Army Hall stood at the top of Bolts Hill where the houses known as The Roundels now stand

## A Disturbance at the Sally Army Hall

One person who does not appear on the census is **James Coltham**, but we know that he was living in the area by 1895, as his name appears in The Whitstable Times and Herne Bay Herald in connection with an altercation at The Salvation Army Hall on 23rd June 1895 along with a William Marsh. I have found a William Marsh living on Primrose Hill, Chartham in 1891, but this may not be the same person, as Marsh is a common name.

William was accused of riotous and indecent conduct in a place registered for religious worship. George Cook, treasurer of the Salvation Army, was addressing a meeting while William Marsh was in the room attempting to cut a man's hair. William called out loudly "A pint of beer would be very nice now Jack" and repeatedly heckled the speech so that George had to stop. The Captain of the Salvation Army, Alfred Franklin, added that William had attended the service the next day and again disturbed proceedings.

James Coltham, described as a labourer living in Shalmsford Street, and Alfred Cork were called to give evidence, and confirmed that William only spoke in a quiet voice. The judge fined William A £1 plus costs of 19 shillings, or in default of payment, 14 days hard labour.

The court subsequently heard details of James Coltham being drunk and disorderly in Shalmsford Street at 10.50pm on the same day. PC Peacock saw James 'very drunk' and described how 'He had his coat off and wanted to fight an imaginary man.' James called two unnamed witnesses to prove he was not drunk, but this did not help as the bench fined him 5 shillings plus 11 shillings costs. Superintendent Wood said that a gang of young men were causing a great annoyance at Chartham and Shalmsford Street by their disorderly conduct. It is interesting to note that the two parts of the village are listed separately: it is not 'Shalmsford Street, Chartham', but 'Shalmsford Street AND Chartham'. They are clearly still seen as two different villages.

Another name missing from the census is **Harriet Philpott** who lived in Shalmsford Street at the time of her death in 1893. She was 53.

# Conclusion

The daily lives of the people who lived in Shalmsford changed enormously during the reign of Queen Victoria. Families who had survived mainly on bread and vegetables now had access to plentiful, processed food, the railway brought goods and took away produce, homes were heated and lit by coal and electricity rather than wood and leisure time continued to increase.

Having said this, the families who live in the village may not have noticed the small, incremental changes and might conclude that their lives had changed very little. The families who live here today still live within walking distance of parents and grandparents, still attend the village school, use the village shops and are baptised, married and buried in St Mary's Church. Families intermarry, and there are few of the original families who are not now related to one another in some distant way.

The story of Shalmsford is the story of countless villages across Kent, the south of England and indeed, across the UK. Location, availability of food and occupations may vary, but people do not. We all want the best for our families and strive to provide a good life for those we love.

This history of Shalmsford is a cameo of life in Britain, showing us that we are not so very different from those who lived here 150 years ago, nor from those who will follow us. The life of a rural village is important and we should recognise and embrace it, counting our blessings while we can.

# Family Trees

The information from the both the census and parish records is very much open to interpretation, with people misremembering birthdates, or indeed deliberately giving false information. There is the added complication of the duplication of names across generations and through alternated branches of a family tree.

To help us make some sense of the people listed above, I have compiled some family tree data. This is taken from the census and from some family information, and I must stress that I hold no confidence that it is 100% accurate. The girl who lied about her age to get married, the semi-illiterate man who left one of his children off the census return and the woman who listed an illegitimate child as that of her late husband all muddy the waters and leave false clues.

I have added the tables for you in case you are interested, but if you are a serious genealogist, please check all the facts against your own research; this can only be considered as preliminary research.

# The Vincer Family Tree

Stephen Vincer (1775-1826) married Elizabeth Cobb (1791-?) and they had six children:

1. Esther Vincer (1823-1893) had one illegitimate child, Eliza (1848. Eliza married Henry Wright and their children were Eliza, Caroline, Henry and Mary.
2. Elizabeth Vincer (1809-1861) also had an illegitimate child, Charles Ruck Vincer (1831-1910), who married Eliza Foster and had three children; Charles, Jane and Stephen.
3. Francer Vincer , too, had a child out of wedlock, Eliza Vincer (1840-1852) before marrying Joseph Spillett. It is reasonable to assume that the child was Joseph's. The couple had one daughter, Jemima Spillett (1846-1847) before Joseph died. Frances' last child, George Spillett (1843) was born too long after Joseph's death to have been his. Frances' daughter Eliza had one illegitimate child, Mary Elizabeth (1869).
4. Stephen Vincer (1811)
5. Maria Vincer (1819-1906) had two illegitimate children, Betsey Vincer (1845-1814) and Ann Maria Vincer (1863-1930). Both daughters had illegitimate children of their own. Betsey had Frances M. E. Vincer (1875-1946) and Ann had Maria Jane E.
6. Mary Vincer (1825-1848) had one illegitimate child, Stephen Vincer (1843-1843).

# The Link Family Tree

William Link (1780) married Maria (1773)

| James (1805-1878) married Jane Partis (1810-1885) | William (1802-1868) married Hannah Taylor (1800) |
|---|---|
| 1. James (1829 -1906) had Henry (1845), William (1852), James (1859)<br>2. Ann (1830-1913) married William Fisher and had Hester (1852-54), James (1856), John (1858), Charles (1861), Edward (1871) and Clara (1871-72)<br>3. Charlotte (1831-1848)<br>4. George (1833-1836)<br>5. John (1833-1912) married Ann (1819) had Emily (1862), Sarah (1865), Thomas, (1870), William (1837-1837)<br>6. Sarah (1838)<br>7. Maria (1840-1909) married William Mumford<br>8. Edward (1844)<br>9. Henry (1844-1879)<br>10. George (1849) married Annie Rogers had Frank<br>11. Jane (1851-1944) married Thomas Cavill Newton<br>12. William (1851-1928) had James (1867), Charles (1873) and Henry (1880) | 1. William (1825)<br>2. Charlotte (1828-1908) married Thomas Finch<br>3. John (1831-1903) married Mary Ann (1832) had William (1851),James (1856) and Edward (1860)<br>4. Henry (1833) married Ann<br>5. Maria (1835)<br>6. James (1837)<br>7. Rachel (1841)<br>8. Edward (1844) married Lydia Philpott (1841) who had William, Louisa (1874), Charles (1877) James (1879), Sidney (1881) and Henry (1883)<br>9. George (1846-1917) married Mary Ann Harris (1850) who had Benjamin, Charles, Emily, Frank |

# Hoare Family Tree

Thomas Hoare married Sarah and had two children.

Firstly, Thomas (1776) married Elizabeth Uden and had a daughter called Elizabeth (1813).

Secondly, Richard (1780-1860) who married Phoebe Benton (1880-1842). Their children were:

1. George (1803-1892) married Mary Back (1804-1887) who had a daughter called Elizabeth (1813 -1897). She married James Austen
2. Richard (1805-1894) married Elizabeth Dodd (1812-1897)and their children were Mary, Ann, Ellen, James, Elizabeth and Charlotte
3. John (1809-1879) married Sarah Ann Austen


1. George Hoare( 1803-1892) married Mary Back (1804-1887)

   a. James (1828- 1853)
   b. Phoebe (1830) married Henry Spillett?
   c. Mary Ann (1832)
   d. Sophia (1834) married Henry Spillett (1830) –
   e. Harriet (1836) married John Gipson (1838) and had Sarah Ann (1857) John (1860), George Henry (1863), James (1878), Mary Ann (1859), Elizabeth (1861)
   f. Ellen 1837 married Archley Harlow 1836- and had six children, George, Sarah Ann, Mary Ann, John, Elizabeth, James. Mary Ann married John Newton
   g. George (1839) married Louisa Linkin and had a child called Alice Martha
   h. Sarah (1841)
   i. Emma (1846) married James Spillett (1844)- had Frederick, Herbert, Rhoda, Ada, Charlotte
   j. John (1847-1847


2. Richard Hoare(1805-1894) married Elizabeth Dodd (1812-1897) and their children were:

   a. John (1833)
   b. Sarah Jane (1835)
   c. Richard (1836)

- d. James Mitchell (1838)- married Emma Mumford had Ann (1863), Fanny (1864), Mitchell (1866), Alfred (1867), Elizabeth (1871), Fred, Ellen (1877)
- e. Phoebe (1840)- married Edward Mumford and had Richard (1862), William(1865) and Lucy (1871)
- f. Frances (1843-43)
- g. Twins Ann (1848)- and Harriet (1848-1848)
- h. Jesse (1843) married
    1. Louisa Reynolds (1841-1880) and had
        Harry (1864) who married Elizabeth and had Edith (1889), Arthur (1891), Louisa, Gilbert, Clara Mabel, Alfred and Isabel
        Emily (1866) who married Isaac Linkin and had Robert, Ada, Henry, Charles, Hilda and Stanley
        Annie (1868)
        George (1871)
        Jesse (1874)
        Edward (1875)
        Rosa (1878) who married Alfred Harlow and had Rosa
    2. Jane E. Pay (1848) and had
        Flora (1883)
        Ernest (1886)
        May (1889)

3.John Hoare (1809-1879) married Sarah Ann Austen (1820-1904)

- a. William (1856) married Emma Down (1856-1814) who had Robert (1880).,Frances (1883),Mabel (1888)
- b. Henry (1845) married Mary Ann Eastland Blackman and had Caroline (1868), Emily (1870),William (1874), Harry (1877), Thomas (1880), Arthur (1882) and Alfred (1885)
- c. Emily married James Vidgen in 1876 and had Arthur (1887), Elizabeth, William (1868) , Ethel (1871-71), Edith (1889)
- d. Edward (1847) married Harriet Vidgen (1848) and had Harriette (1870), William (1872), Walter (1875), Minnie (1878), Frederick (1879)
- e. Frederick (1858)
- f. John (1866)
- g. Jane (1850)

# The Hukins Family Tree

Ambrose Hukins (1750-1837) married Elizabeth Burchett (d. 1850)
and their children were:
1) Ambrose (1864)
2) Thomas (1790-1864) married Mary Ann Hall (1794) and had Ambrose (1834), James (1831), Thomas (1832-1855), Charles (1836) and Harriet (1841)
    Secondly, married Marianne Stubberfield (1818) and adopted her son James Stubberfield (1850)
3) Philip (1799) married Catherine Edmonds (1867) and had William (1838)
4) Jesse (1801- 1882) married Elizabeth Christian (1806) and had the following children:
    a. Sarah (1827) married Edward Keeler (1821-1882) and had Jesse (1852), Alfred (1855), Walter (1858) and Norris (1860)
    b. Elizabeth (1831)
    c. Jesse (1833)
    d. Philip (1836)
    e. William (1838)
    f. Ann (1841)
    g. Lucy (1842)
    h. Mary Jane (1844-1937)
    i. Fred (1847)
    j. Edward (1854-58)

# The Spillett Family Tree

Thomas Spillett (1787-1870) married Jemima (1790-1847)

1. Edward (1809) married Mary Parker had Henry (1819) * married Phoebe Hogben (1826-70), Mary (1821) married Charles (1814), George (1834) **married Harriet Jarvis (1837)
2. Thomas (1811) married Sarah Russell (1814) and had Thomas (1844), Phoebe (1830-1849), Frank (1854), James (1854)
3. William (1812)
4. George (1814) married Charlotte Gibson (1817) had James (1843), George (1845), Fredrick (1862)
5. Stephen (1816) married Caroline Dale (1823) had Eliza (1848-48), Martha (1844-48), Martha (1849), Hester (1845), Edwin (1854), Sophia (1856)
6. Joseph (1821-1847) married Frances Vincer (1820) and had Eliza (1840) and George (1854) (George is not Joseph's child )
7. Frederick (1828) married Ann (1827) had Eliza (1851)
8. Henry (1828) married Sophie Hoare (1825)
9. William (1828) married Mary Richardson and had Jeanette (1864), Charlotte (1854) and Elizabeth (1857)
10. John (1833) married Ann (1822) had Frances, Herbert, Mary, Ernest

| * Henry (1819) married Phoebe (1826) | **George (1834) and Harriet (1837) |
|---|---|
| 1. John (1847) | 1. John (1858) |
| 2. Henry (1852) | 2. Edward (1858) |
| 3. George (1857) | 3. George (1860) |
| 4. Edwin (1860) | 4. William (1865) |
| 5. Phoebe (1863) | 5. Mary Jane (1867) |
| 6. James (1865) | 6. Edith (1870 |
| 7. Alfred (1868) | 7. Edgar (1871) |
|  | 8. Frederick (1876) |

# Bibliography

'A Saunter Through Kent with Pen and Pencil', Charles Igglesden, Kentish Express, 1933
'Chartham and Its Church', Graham Haslam, Gordon Luc, 1987
'Chartham Hatch – from village school to village school', The History Project Group of The Chartham Hatch Village Hall Society, 2007
'Chartham in Days of Old', Selina Randolf, 1911
'Domestic Bygones', Jacqueline Fearn, Shire Publications Ltd, 1977
'Farm Waggons and Carts', James Arnold, David and Charles, 1977
'Forgotten Household Crafts', John Seymour, The National Trust, 1996
'How to be a Victorian', Ruth Goodman, Viking Books, 2013
'Kent 1800-1899 – a chronicle of the nineteenth century', Bob Ogley, Froglets Publications, 2003
'Kent Dialect', Ian Howe, Bradwell Books, 2012
'Kent of one hundred years ago', Aylwin Guilmant, Alan Sutton, 1997
'Kent Railways', David Staines, Countryside Books, 2010
'My Ancestor was an Agricultural Labourer', Ian H. Waller, Society of Geneologists Enterprises Ltd, 2014
'Occupational Costume in England', Phillis Cunningham & Catherine Lucas, A & C Black, 1976
'Old Farms – an illustrated guide' John Viner, John Murray, 1982
'Rural Britain Then and Now', Roger Hunt, Cassell Illustrated,- 2004
'Tales of the Old Woodlanders', Valerie Porter, David & Charles, 1995
'The Butterfly Book of Kentish Recipes', Susan Hibberd, The DIggory Press, 2008
'The English Farmhouse and Cottage', M.W. Barley, Routledge & Kegan Paul, 1976
'The English Village', Richard Muir, Thames and Hudson, 1980
'The Truth About Cottages', John Woodforde, Routledge & Kegan Paul, 1980

www.ingramcontent.com/pod-product-compliance
Lightning Source LLC
Chambersburg PA
CBHW081013040426
42444CB00014B/3189